BUILDING
A BUSINESS
the Buddhist Way

BUILDING
A BUSINESS
the Buddhist Way

A PRACTITIONER'S GUIDEBOOK

G E R I L A R K I N

CELESTIALARTS
Berkeley, California

Celestial Arts
P.O. Box 7123
Berkeley, California 94707

Distributed in Canada by Ten Speed Canada, in the United
Kingdom and Europe by Airlift Books, in New Zealand by
Tandem Press, in Australia by Simon & Schuster Australia,
in South Africa by Real Books, and in Singapore, Malaysia,
Hong Kong, and Thailand by Berkeley Books.

Cover and interior design by Greene Design
Cover photograph by Chantra Pramkaew

Library of Congress Catalog Card Number: 99-72209

First printing, 1999
Printed in the United States

1 2 3 4 5 6 7 8 — 03 02 01 00 99

Dedication

This book is dedicated to all of you who have the courage to embrace right livelihood as the framework for your life's work and, in particular, to Ann and Jackie Perrault-Victor, who continue to cultivate new ground in this spiritual-work-meets-financial-success realm.

Contents

Introduction

"Life is too short to be a jerk!" Fighting words. The eighty-year-old who was whispering them to me was an old-time union organizer based in Midland, Michigan, home of Dow Chemical. His choice of livelihood had not been an easy one. But it worked for him, gave his life meaning, kept the twinkle in his eyes that lit up any room he walked into.

I had driven three hours before dawn to get to the city in time to start an intense strategic planning retreat for the women's shelter there. Hearing stories about domestic violence is always excruciatingly painful—even when it is about a Midland woman who whacks her husband on the head with an iron frying pan every time he decides to go off for sex with one of the neighbors. After a tedious morning filled with statistics of what had become a fast-growing problem in these parts, I found myself sitting next to the old lion at lunch. He had made the mistake of asking me about my life. As I whined my way through the personal costs of management consulting, I asked for his opinion about a particular problem that was driving me nuts. This was it: I kept getting clients—entrepreneurs—who were looking for business training that would embrace their personal values while they learned the nuts and bolts of building a business. And they couldn't find any. Even worse, the business owners who insisted on trying to integrate their values with their businesses on their own—training deprived—were having a terrible time finding financing. Mostly it was that they kept flunking the question, "How many hours do you spend at work each week?" Since balancing business hours with family time was a top priority for this group, they weren't spending the accepted norm of sixty to seventy hours at their desks. From an investor's perspective it wasn't enough. They were stuck. I was stuck. I had no idea how to help any of them.

At that, the old guy looked me in the eye and grinned, "For Chrissakes, start your own training. You'll know what to do."

So I did. With the blessings of my teachers, I organized a curriculum based on almost twenty years of working with growing companies and merged it with lessons I had learned during my three years as a Zen Buddhist seminarian. Started the training. Put together a financing pool for young companies. It took a while to pull the pieces together: sessions that were lean but comprehensive, a place people could get to using public transportation, a sponsor. The banks turned me down but Whole Foods (yes, the grocery company) didn't. "Building a Business the Zen Way" became a wildly successful training program that cut to the essential questions we all need to think through if we are to do the work that matches who we are. For example:

- What are our real values?

- What is our vision for how we want to live our lives?

- What skills and talents do we bring to this vision?

- Based on our skills and talents, what can we sell that incorporates our values and still makes money?

The last question raises an important point. The Buddha never taught that poverty is valuable in and of itself. His family was very wealthy, and some of his best friends were kings. It's just fine to make money—as long as it's good money. The trick is to make it in a way that honors the universe (and to share the money). In the Buddhist tradition in which I have been trained, we are advised to live on about a third of what we make, to save a third for old age, and to share a third.

Most importantly, since we started this training I've realized that *Building a Business the Buddhist Way* is about radical honesty—yours—and how that honesty has the power not only to help you to sort through livelihood possibilities but also to add momentum to your spiritual path, whatever it is. Work practice is one of the most powerful spiritual practices available to each of us.

Right livelihood is also about simplifying your life. It provides an excuse for letting go of the things that aren't working, of the values that aren't your own. In that letting go a spaciousness is created that gives you mental and emotional room for creating the life you want, for responding quickly to market opportunities, for rapidly addressing the people problems that invariably surface as businesses grow. The irony of this path is that radically honest businesses, businesses of integrity, businesses that respect and cherish all beings, succeed. Getting to that success simply takes knowing what steps to take and having the tools you need. Those two things are exactly what this workbook is all about. Steps and tools.

The very heart of right livelihood is where our values merge with work. Happily, there are many examples of this flavor of business all around us. Sometimes it's what people sell: clothing made from organically grown cotton. Sometimes it's how policies are structured: an entire team interviews a candidate before she is hired, because managers respect their wisdom about who will best fit into their rhythm. Sometimes it's how clients are treated: telling the truth about whether a deadline can be met. In the best examples, right livelihood businesses have all three of these qualities—products that are protective of the earth and its inhabitants, policies that assume staff are deeply valuable to a company, and compassionately honest client interactions. The karmic jackpot.

Here's one example of a business that oozes right livelihood themes. In Ann Arbor there is an extraordinary deli, Zingermans, that does more business per square foot than almost anybody anywhere. Enough for the national media to stand up and take notice. And while I dream of their brownies during every full moon, to me the amazing thing about Zingermans is the percentage of profits they put back into staff support in the form of benefits, wages, profit sharing, and funding for staff-initiated entrepreneurial projects. The owners have even seeded independent businesses started by their staff. One of them is the best bakery in town.

Here's another example of a right livelihood business. Suzanne Meade is an extraordinary cellist. She grew up in Neenah, Wisconsin, a spunky, beautiful redheaded kid who was valedictorian of her high school. Today she teaches cello. But there's more. Suzanne uses her teaching as a vehicle for instilling self-esteem, wisdom, and peacefulness in her students. Instead of pressure, here is how she talks to her students about practicing: "Get a realistic picture in your mind of what you do with your time during the day. What do you have to do, like to do, have no control over, or have some say about? Break it down into a general chart—what and when. (Eating, homework, friends, vegetating, etc.) It will take two minutes. Then, *this is the clincher,* pick the time that is the least painful and most likely to survive based on you and your tendencies. Be kind...Take the long term approach. I mean *long*! Pablo Casals said that the secret to his ability to put in lots of enjoyable practice was that he always imagined he had forever to work it out." Suzanne's students perform well, love playing, and have a remarkable calmness about them relative to their music. Her compassion and integrity are obvious in their efforts.

How can you shift your own livelihood so that it better reflects your deepest ethical values? First, admit this: you are yearning for something more in your life or you would *never* have read this far. There are too many other things to do. The yearning is healthy and healing, and will provide the tenacity you'll need to see your new work into fruition. A business of integrity feeds our deepest hungers. It is a vehicle for connecting deeply with the creative spirit of our lives and provides a way for each of us to express our unique gifts and talents. It offers the proof we need that each of our lives matters. Finally, it is proof that work can give each of us a sense of joy.

This workbook has largely been written for beginners, for people who have decided that they want to commit themselves to living a life of integrity and are searching for clues about where to start. Having said this, old-timers will find revisiting some of the sections very useful as well. We forget a lot, you and I.

There are six chapters following this introduction. The first one outlines the characteristics of a right livelihood business. It starts with precepts, principles to base our lives on. Not to lie or steal. To consider all things precious. A formula for balancing our lives is offered because right livelihood businesses are best nurtured by people whose lives are balanced. Finally, I make a heartfelt plea for taking the long view and letting your business unfold at its own pace.

The second chapter, "What Is Your Path?", is about figuring out, once and for all, what your purpose is in this lifetime. Time is running out for all of us. It is critical not to waste any part of what is left, even if what is left could stretch out for another eighty years. "What Is Your Path?" offers an opportunity to be honest about what you have loved doing, and what you have hated. It also has some exercises that are useful for reflecting on what really matters to you the most. Ironically, you and I typically try to cram as much as possible into our lives instead of zooming in on what really matters and immersing ourselves in that.

Chapter Three offers some preliminary insights into what it means to be an entrepreneur who is embarking on a right livelihood path. The core activities that make up the transition to entrepreneur are outlined, and a self-assessment, as in "Can I Really Do This?!" is included. You'll also find an exercise aimed at helping you sort through any fears that may have you frozen in place right about now.

Chapter Four summarizes the business plan, a must for any business of integrity. Why? Because it steers you toward wisdom, efficiency, and effectiveness as you watch how your business could unfold if you choose a particular path. A business plan doesn't have to be long and it doesn't need to be fancy, but it does need to be thoughtful and thorough. What a business plan is, why it is critical to you (I carry mine around in my pocket-sized calendar for easy reference), and its parts are all included.

Marketing is the focus of Chapter Five. In some ways it is a basic marketing class clothed in Zen precepts. It starts out with a discussion of context because what is happening around us has a huge impact on our business potential. So we might as well face context up front, like a true warrior. Next is customers: who they are and where they are and what we have to do to reach them. Competition (and how to compete without worrying if you will end up in hell from some dastardly competitive moves) can be found in this chapter. I've also included some tougher concepts like positioning.

The tip of the iceberg that is marketing is all we can cover in this workbook. But it will be enough to give you a head start. Happily there are libraries full of excellent marketing books that can guide you through the everyday details of selling. If you find yourself thirsty for more and want a basic "how-to," check out *Twelve Simple Steps to a Winning Marketing Plan* (Probus, 1992). It's dry but useful. I wrote it for my consulting clients in a pique of frustration when I couldn't find a basic marketing book to buy for them.

The last chapter, Chapter Six, is about money. You'll need it. You'll need money to start your business (even if just enough to pay your monthly bills) and you'll need it to grow your business. A cash flow worksheet is offered as a model for keeping track of expenses and income. Even when your business is seething with integrity, a lack of income gets tiresome early. Fortunately, as we shift millenniums, we have access to excellent software capable of performing all of the mundane tasks associated with tracking your finances. So if your first purchase after you finish this workbook is a business phone, your second one needs to be a computer complete with accounting software you can understand. So you can use it. So you never, ever end up in jail because you didn't pay all the taxes you owed.

Just so you know, miracles happen. Here's one. The Cass Corridor of Detroit is perceived as a canker sore in the heart of the inner city by many of us Michigan people, mostly run-down and trashed. Homeless residents share the streets with students and other low-income Detroiters, many of them barely eking out an existence. It is dangerous, this corridor. Dirty. Scary after dark and sometimes in the sunshine.

Jackie Victor and Ann Perrault decided that Cass was a perfect place for a bakery. Not only that, they were determined to make only the highest quality breads—all organic—and to hire people from the neighborhood as staff: "We want to .... create a safe oasis in a sorely neglected area of the city, and we're committed to organic because it's good for the earth." The two picked a spot in the middle of a tough block, apprenticed as bakers at Stone House Breads, a respected European-style bakery in northern Michigan, wrote a business plan, and managed to raise enough money from banks, friends, and family to open their doors.

Then we all held our collective breath while Jackie and Ann worked around the clock. We watched for graffiti. For break-ins. For theft. For drugs. For the project to be abandoned. Instead, several homeless men began to patrol the block to make sure the bakery stayed unharmed.

Neighborhood residents were hired. And orders came in. They came in with such enthusiasm that a year after opening their doors, the two women had fifteen employees and enough profit to pay off their start-up loans. If they can, you can. Before they started, Ann and Jackie thought long and hard about how they could create jobs in the city. And they thought long and hard about the needs of the residents: for respect, for work, for community. And then, homework completed, they just started—and kept going while the rest of us, jaws dropped, stood by and applauded their tenacity and deeply held ethics.

There are several ways to move through this workbook. If you are taking the course, "Building a Business the Zen Way," in Ann Arbor or New York, the instructor will guide you through the chapters and offer instructions regarding each worksheet. If you aren't able to attend the course because you live too far away or because we have all suddenly decided to pack it up and spend the rest of our days in a cave, I heartily recommend that you read through the entire workbook front to back before you fill in any of the worksheets. Then go back and do the work-sheets chapter by chapter with as much thoughtfulness, clarity, and honesty as you can muster. It will lead to a better business. My hope is that each one of you—having completed all of the exercises—will have planned and started to implement a business of integrity by the time you reach the last worksheet, or will have moved your existing business further along your spiritual path. I hope the result will be a business that honors you, the people around you, and the universe at large. Good luck—and try not to act too surprised when you're wildly successful, OK? That is *so* 1990s.

A deep bow from your dharma sister,

Geri Larkin
February 1999
Ann Arbor, Michigan

✳

Chapter One

The Characteristics of Right Livelihood Businesses

For years I wrestled with the age-old dilemma of whether I could make good money and still live a life of integrity. Lots of books were saying "yes," but I wasn't seeing it in practice back then, since The Social Venture Network, with members like Ben and Jerry's and Tommy Boy Music, hadn't yet surfaced. I couldn't find any business leaders who pledged to "create a more just, humane, and environmentally sustainable society," as some are saying today. And I looked. As a management consultant, my experience was that good money was only made in BIG companies, in growing companies, in companies that weren't treating the world or their people all that well, thank you very much. And yes, some of it was intentional but most of it wasn't. My friends who were making good money were often exhausted, cranky more often than was healthy, stressed in the extreme, and spending an inordinate amount of time trying to remember the names of their kids.

In 1991, as a card-carrying member of the good-money-and-stressed-in-the-extreme club, my desperate search for calm led me to join the Maitreya Buddhist Seminary as a student. Somewhere in the middle of the three-year program, I realized that all things are possible. That we could, each of us, make good money *and* live a life of integrity. That realization was a personal green light. It gave me permission to start exploring, to admit that I was yearning for something different. I started exploring right livelihood, and the more I looked, the more I knew I was home.

SPIRITUAL PRINCIPLES

A right livelihood business has several outstanding characteristics. The bottom line is one of principles. Right livelihood businesses do not make money just to make money. They don't drive their staff into the ground, or market to everyone, everywhere, wasting valuable resources—time, human energy, paper, postage, cyberspace. These are businesses that hold all things as precious in the same way you or I would if we knew we would be dead tomorrow. They embrace balance, acknowledging that energy and creativity flow naturally out of well-rounded lifestyles. Patience is considered a virtue: these are long-haul businesses (even if they are owned by different players over time), and they are businesses that refuse to justify incremental growth instead of cyberspeed growth. Common sense merges with ethical values. And the icing on the cake? Fun. Right livelihood businesses are just plain fun. Humor is always present, along with a refreshing humility. "We'll do our best and see how it plays out, knowing and openly admitting that we don't control the universe."

In my experience the characteristic that best separates right livelihood businesses from the rest of the pack is that they are driven by spirituality-based principles. These might come in the form of commandments or in the embracing of the teachings of the ancient Judaic mystics. For me, the Buddhist precepts offer one user-friendly framework that has served many of my clients well over the years. While there are many versions of the core precepts, Thich Nhat Hanh's version has always struck me as having a clarity useful in the day-to-day business decisions we all face. There are five precepts:

1. *I am committed to cultivating compassion and learning ways to protect the lives of people, animals, plants, and minerals. I am determined not to kill, not to let others kill, and not to condone any act of killing in the world, in my thinking, and in my way of life.*

2. *I am committed to cultivating loving kindness and learning ways to work for the well-being of people, animals, plants, and minerals. I*

vow to practice generosity by sharing my time, energy, and material resources with those who are in real need. I am determined not to steal and not to possess anything that should belong to others. I will respect the property of others, but I will prevent others from profiting from human suffering or the suffering of other species on Earth.

3. I am committed to cultivating responsibility and learning ways to protect the safety and integrity of individuals, couples, families, and society. I am determined not to engage in sexual relations without love and a long-term commitment. To preserve the happiness of myself and others, I am determined to respect my commitments and the commitments of others. I will do everything in my power to protect children from sexual abuse and to prevent couples and families from being broken by sexual misconduct.

4. I am committed to cultivating loving speech and deep listening in order to bring joy and happiness to others and relieve others of their suffering. Knowing that words can create happiness or suffering, I am determined to speak truthfully, with words that inspire self-confidence, joy, and hope. I will not spread news that I do not know to be certain and will not criticize or condemn things of which I am not sure. I will refrain from uttering words that can cause division or discord, or that can cause the family or community to break. I am determined to make all efforts to reconcile and resolve all conflicts, however small.

5. I am committed to cultivating good health, both physical and mental, for myself, my family, and my society by practicing mindful eating, drinking, and consuming. I will ingest only items that preserve peace, well-being, and joy in my body, in my consciousness, and in the collective body and consciousness of my family and society. I am determined not to use any alcohol or any intoxicant or to ingest foods or other items that contain toxins, such as certain TV programs, magazines, books, films, and conversations. I am aware that to damage my body or my consciousness with these poisons is to

betray my ancestors, my parents, my society, and future generations. I will work to transform violence, fear, anger, and confusion in myself and in society by practicing a diet for myself and for society. I understand that a proper diet is crucial for self-transformation and for the transformation of society.

(Taken from Thich Nhat Hanh's *For a Future to be Possible,* Parallax Press, 1993, pp. 3–5)

Here's why I've always turned to precepts as a framework for running a business. Unlike commandments, which are directives, the precepts are our intentions for ourselves, our businesses, and our environment. As such, we do the best we can. When we stumble, rather than feeling guilty, our job is to pick ourselves up, make amends as best as we are able, and pick up where we left off.

BALANCE

Precepts such as the ones offered in this workbook are a useful place to begin when you think about building a business of integrity, and the place to go back to when things feel off-kilter...which brings me to balance. We can still embrace the precepts and get sucked into our business like a dust ball into a vacuum cleaner. Meanwhile, we need to keep our energy up and our creativity quotient high for our enterprise to prosper and grow. Balance is what keeps us sane. It feeds our energy level. Without it, we're goners. Workaholism does not work in right livelihood businesses. It's too one-dimensional. What we may gain in focus, we lose in tracking the broader context within which we are trying to build a business. When our work is everything, it can cost us our families, our friends, and eventually the business itself. Many times I have watched entrepreneurs work around the clock to build their businesses, only to come up for air five years later to a divorce and a market that has shifted right out from under them. Unwise, this one-dimensional life. We need to define what balance means for us, and to embrace it, both in our own lives and in the lives of our staff, clients (which means *not* calling them on weekends or at night unless they ask), suppliers, and other stakeholders.

So a second characteristic of a right livelihood business is that it acknowledges and embraces *all* of the aspects of our lives. It respects that we are not just our business but have other components in our days that matter to us—families that need us, friends, culture, spirituality, play.

In their book, *Instructions to the Cook,* Bernard Glassman and Rick Fields better explain what I am trying to say. In Zen Buddhism, living a full life is often described as "living the supreme meal." Dogen, the thirteenth-century founder of the Japanese Soto Zen tradition, first introduced the concept in his own teachings to his students. He taught that one of the most useful metaphors for a life well lived is what happens in the kitchen. In other words, a full life is like a full-course meal.

Living our lives as a supreme meal means admitting to ourselves that we need more than one "course," more than just our work. For Glassman, a fully-lived life has five courses. The first is our own spirituality. This provides us with an unending stream of energy and meaning. In Glassman's words, our spirituality helps us to realize the oneness of life and provides the still point at the center of all of the things we do in a day. To be fed by this course, we need to do our spiritual practice—whether it is meditation, prayer, walking in the woods, dancing, or just being alone in a quiet place. And we need to do it regularly. Every single day.

The second course of our life is study or learning; not just book study, but mastery of new skills or adventures into new places. It's getting to know new people, people we might not otherwise know—from different cultures, different ages, other sexes. Study gives us sharpness and keeps our minds working. It feeds our curiosity and rewards our risking new places, people, and things. It also keeps us young and fresh and interesting.

How we make our living is the third course. In the best circumstances it builds on the first two courses, on spiritual practice and study. It is the part of our meal that keeps us going in the physical world: "It is the course of work and business—the meat and potatoes. Taking care of ourselves and making a living in the world are necessary and important for all of us, no matter how 'spiritual' we may think we are." (*Instructions to the Cook: A Zen Master's Lessons in Living a Life that Matters,* by Bernard Glassman and Rick Fields. Bell Tower, New York, 1996, p.8) What is important to remember is that while our work is important, it is only one portion of our life.

The fourth course is called social action. I call it doing good. When Buddha was giving dharma talks almost three thousand years ago, he would tell people that it was not really worth teaching them anything about becoming more spiritual until they got really skilled at being generous. My own experience is that the man was on to something. Not only that—without generosity it is virtually impossible to run a right livelihood business because we become too "self" focused and, in the extreme, too greedy. So we need to do good. It can be spontaneous and informal. Bending over to pick up trash. Tucking some extra cash into the pocket of someone you know is running low. And it can be formal. Donating time to programs like Habitat for Humanity or Amnesty International. Agreeing to be a board member for a local nonprofit organization. The list is endless.

The last course is the course of relationship and community. Dessert! We need relationships. Friends and family. We need community. Without them our loneliness can seep into all of the other courses of our lives, turning them into mold and mush. The last course is the one that weaves all of the other courses together into an honest-to-goodness work of art. A feast worth living.

As you begin a business or start to steer an existing business on to a different course, what matters is remembering that our work needs to feed and to be fed by the other courses of our supreme meal.

USING THE RESOURCES YOU HAVE

The third characteristic of a right livelihood business has to do with resources. Most westerners are taught that it is critical to gather significant resources about us before we embark on building a business, whether we are starting from scratch or expanding. I believed that for years. What I have learned, however, is almost the opposite. You can start with what you have, where you are. The role of the resources you are able to gather for the business is simply to tell you *what the scale of the business or expansion will be.* That's all. In other words, will you bring a management consultant in to help you shift your business toward a right livelihood business, or will a small group of "believers" have to sweat it out at weekly breakfast meetings over the next year? Will the breakfast meetings be in a restaurant or will they be pot luck? Will they be pot luck or will you be eating yesterday's bagels donated by a local bagel factory? The outcome of your efforts will be the same.

If you are starting a business, the resources you can access simply tell you whether you will be starting the business as a part-time operation out of your basement, moving into a new office complex complete with technology outlets, a gym, spa, and corner offices, or something in between.

Scale does not define success. And surprisingly, the resources you start out with don't either. In 1996, when we started The Right Livelihood Fund at The Zen Buddhist Temple in Ann Arbor, our first inclination was to put together a budget that included full-time staff, an office, state-of-the-art technologies (I was dying for one of those totally cool handheld Palm Pilots that would organize all of the courses of my own life), and free counseling for all of the training participants. When the three foundations we approached turned us down flat, our first reaction was to say, "Forget it." Fortunately Dogen saved the day: "Start where you are and start with what you have." So we did.

Relying totally on volunteers, donated space, and a couple of small (as in under a thousand dollars) donations, we made a poster, put it up in coffee shops, and started the training. Since then, hundreds of people have gone through our classes. Right livelihood businesses have been started and grown. Existing businesses have totally shifted their focus. Using the fees from the classes, we have been able to invest in a handful of businesses. One of them, the organic bakery in downtown Detroit, already has a dozen employees after only a year in business. Whole Foods, bless their generous hearts, has become a sponsor, making it possible to offer free counseling to some of the lowest income participants. The program is happy, healthy, and strong because we started where we were and worked with what we had.

PATIENCE

Finally, a right livelihood business is *patient.* It grows in an unforced way, if it grows at all. If it is meant to grow, it grows incrementally in a way that makes it possible for the people involved to continue to embrace the other aspects of their lives. It also grows incrementally so that the environment can be protected and the quality of the business, its products, and its operations can be sustained.

Patience can be very difficult, particularly for those of us with an addiction to caffeine, multitasking, and hyperactivity. And yet it matters. Patience matters because it allows space for a business to take form in a natural, integrative way. Patience lets us monitor the consequences of changes—both intended and unintended—so any negative impacts can be quickly corrected. A right livelihood business is a path—*your* path. Why rush it? Better to wallow in its unfolding, to be excited by its potential, its juiciness. Mastery is the goal here, not profit for profit's sake. Profit for profit's sake is too easy anyway. Why should we waste our lives on linear achievements when there can be so much more?

THE CHARACTERISTICS
OF A RIGHT LIVELIHOOD BUSINESS

1. It embraces principles. The Buddhist precepts are one form and include:

A. _____

_____

_____

_____

_____

B. _____

_____

_____

_____

_____

C. _____

_____

_____

_____

_____

D. _____

_____

_____

_____

_____

E. _____

_____

_____

_____

2. A life of balance is lived as "the supreme meal." It has five courses:

   A. _____

   _____

   _____

   B. _____

   _____

   _____

   C. _____

   _____

   _____

   D. _____

   _____

   _____

   E. _____

   _____

   _____

3. We need to start:

   A. _____

   _____

   B. _____

   _____

4. Patience matters.

Chapter Two

What Is Your Path?

---

*" I just want to love my work so it is not a mat-
ter of having work and having fun and being
able to do things. I want it all to fit together.
That is one of the reasons I want to start my own
company, so at least it will be my thing, my passion. And it will be a part of my whole life, so
my life and my family all fit into one."*

(Focus group participant in San Francisco,
Details *magazine, 1996)*

Jill Blixt is my hero. When I first moved to Ann Arbor, Michigan almost
twenty years ago, I kept hearing about this advertising firm, Blixt and
Associates—mostly when I went to fancy parties with my wealthiest
friends in town. It was one of the city's "hot" companies. Run by a wife-
and-husband team, Blixt and Associates had a reputation for being edgy,
creative, and choosy about its clients. When we used their services during my tenure as a management consultant at Deloitte and Touche, I got
to know Jill and Al Blixt personally and tried not to be a groupie. Then,
years later, they said good-bye to a major client, one who was brutally
difficult to work with. In no time at all they faced a major financial crisis

11

when their bank suddenly decided that without the client they were a financial risk. Loans were pulled. The two almost lost everything—including their house. Al, an attorney and a natural coach, began consulting on issues relating to organizational change. And Jill had the courage to sit still long enough to really think about what matters to her. She inventoried her strengths and skills and decided that she wanted to live her days very differently. So she metamorphed from Jill Blixt, ad agency owner to Jill Blixt, creativity coach. Today she helps clients tap into their deepest selves, where they discover a mother lode of creativity.

The backbone of her work is a series of four courses that provide a safe haven for people like you and me to bring to the surface what we need in order to get the stream started. My favorite is a one-day workshop, "Mothers and Daughters: Believing Mirrors." Here's a description of it: "There's so much mothers and daughters can offer each other. But too often they get caught up in negative self-talk and beliefs that they are never enough. This workshop ...help(s) them open communication, see each other with new eyes, and become powerful 'believing mirrors.'" I took my daughter and learned more about her in one afternoon than I could ever have hoped—her dreams, her fears, what still makes her mad, how funny she is. Jill found her path and now helps the rest of us to rediscover not just ourselves but each other. Right livelihood.

In a recent interview in *Inc.* magazine, Lanny Goodman, a well known and widely respected management consultant, argued vehemently that a business has to satisfy your needs to succeed. Somewhere around fifty years old, more than six feet tall, bespectacled, tea connoisseur, ponytailed—Goodman has started many successful businesses. He has been a jeweler, a sailmaker, a personality profiler, a consultant. He is a sought-after keynote speaker who regularly turns his audiences upside down. Based on his own experience, he teaches that businesses have to match their owners to succeed and that the owners have to think of themselves first. He instructs entrepreneurs to constantly ask themselves four key questions:

1. What do I need and want out of life?
2. How can my company accomplish that?
3. What would such a company look like?
4. How do I/we get it to look like that?

"Listen to what (business owners) say even if they do think they have conscious plans and goals: 'I want to grow 10% a year.' 'I want to take the company to the next level.' Who cares? Explain to me why that matters. Ask most CEO's for that kind of an explanation and they can't give you one....by the time a company gets past start-up and establishes that it can survive, most founders are so used to being reactive that it doesn't occur to them to reflect on their own .... We lose sight of the fact that we live better than the pharaohs. Does it really matter if we make $1 million, $5 million, or $50 million? So the real question is: how can I create a life that I will look back on as an incredible shining adventure, and how can the business be a vehicle to help me accomplish that?" (*Inc.*, January, 1998, p. 66)

Goodman gets it. Our real job is to live a life that is an incredible shining adventure. The place to start is inside of ourselves. When we're alone and staring out a window we can ask ourselves the questions that really matter to us. What are our real values? What are we honestly good at—because we love doing it? And how does all of this translate into our own path?

We each have our own path. After forty-something years of living on this spunky planet we all call home I am convinced of this truth. I remember at Deloitte and Touche, where I was one of the staff who worked with emerging businesses, how I could almost always pick out the potential clients who were going to succeed in their businesses. It wasn't so much that they had convincing business plans, although that was part of it. It was more that the business they wanted to start matched their personality, their values, and their talents—and offered benefits to more than just their customers. Maybe it was profit sharing. Or they were replacing a lost industry in a community. Sometimes it was a much-needed service—recycling printer cartridges or coaching professionals out of dead-end jobs. One of the companies made a family of personal safety products for professional women who travel, things like extra locks for hotel room doors and keys with lights embedded in them. Invariably these were the people who would walk into my office, look at me, and say with an excited, almost quizzical expression, "I know this sounds weird, but all of the pieces of my life have somehow come together in this business."

And if the business was consistent with the precepts, if it had integrity, I knew their success was simply a matter of time. Laurence Boldt, a wise career consultant, describes this phenomenon in a slightly different way:

"There was a time when people accepted being told whom they should marry, and they resigned themselves to making the best of it. Today people expect to marry for love. Most people would frown at the idea of marrying for money. Yet they still feel the need to put money first when thinking about a career. My interest is in helping people uncover their 'life's work' —work that is the most appropriate vehicle for express-ing their most unique talents and abilities. One way I do this is by paying attention to the physical changes they go through as we talk. There's a total transformation in the way clients look and act when they're speak-ing about the things they care for deeply. I think that's an expression of their soul and it holds the clues about where to look for new work."

The first real step in building a business the Buddhist way is to deter-mine your path. And the prestep to that—if there is one—is to tell your-self that you have a moral obligation to live your own path, because it is true. If your path is to be a teacher, teach. If it is to sing, then sing. If it is to be a leader, lead. The good news is that your path, your true path, always has integrity. I don't know why exactly, but I know it is true.

And if you really aren't sure if this is the time to make a change? The "Is It Time?" checklist will help you decide. I actually first saw a version of the checklist on a newsletter from the property management company that keeps my apartment complex up and running. Since then I've run across many more versions, all of them useful. The point is to have the courage to really assess where you are right now so you will have a sense of what it will take to move forward. Such an assessment creates momentum for changes the deepest part of you is ready to embrace.

IS IT TIME?

How satisfied are you with the work you are doing right now? Rate how you *feel* —satisfied (s), dissatisfied (d), or undecided (?)—about your present livelihood in the following areas:

_____ Personal growth and development (Also professional growth and development if it matters to you)

_____ Appropriate salary level

_____ Self-esteem (Self-respect counts here too.)

_____ Participating in decision making

_____ Accomplishing something worthwhile

_____ Amount of authority

_____ Amount of autonomy

_____ Assisting others

_____ Time to pursue other activities (spiritual, leisure, sleep, playing with your pet)

_____ Social status and prestige

_____ Desirable locale (this means close to home—think of protecting the environment)

_____ Opportunity to develop authentic friendships

_____ Varied responsibilities

_____ Seeing real results from your work

_____ Feedback on how you are doing

_____ Fringe benefits

____ Promotions based on merit (as opposed to favoritism, family connections, or worst of all, great legs)

____ A sense of purpose

____ Use of special skills/abilities

____ Respect and support from the people around you

____ Compatibility of personal goals and values with what you are actually doing

____ Adequate resources to do your work

____ Respect and fair treatment

____ Physical surroundings

____ Interesting work

____ Ability to use own ideas

____ Time to spend with family

____ Client/customer appreciation

____ Amount of unrelated/clerical work

____ Having a sense of identity

____ Challenging work

____ Work hours

____ Using creativity

Scoring: Give yourself one point for each S, add no points for each "?", and subtract one point for each D. The higher your score, the more satisfied you are with your livelihood. If you are pretty satisfied you should have twenty-five or more points. The lower the score, the more discontented you are. A score of -5 or worse means it is time to move on.

Here's an extra credit insight: If you suspect that you would have answered this quiz in a similar way six months or even a year ago, you may be in the throes of procrastination. And the stress of your situation may be affecting your health. Think about it, OK? Life is short.

THE CHARACTERISTICS OF A PERSON ON HIS OR HER APPROPRIATE PATH

The characteristics of a person who is on his or her appropriate path are always clear to the people around them. Think for a minute. These are people whose lives are everything they can be. They are living the supreme meal. Their livelihood uses all of the aspects of their personhood, combining interests, skills, and values. And it doesn't matter whether she is the president of a social investment firm or he is a psychiatric nurse, their characteristics are similar.

Lisa Renard was a breathtakingly beautiful eighteen-year-old receptionist for an international corporation when I first met her. Smart as they come. Spunky. Smart aleck-y. Teased a lot. Moved fast. As I got to know her, I learned about her excruciatingly painful childhood and now, even ten years later, I am deeply respectful of her sheer drive for survival. Lisa has tested a number of paths. For awhile she was a computer whiz, a trouble shooter, an Internet queen. Then she started her own marketing firm. She wrote articles and sold them to respected journals.

Then, in her late twenties, the shift happened. She found her path—teaching creative writing to high school kids starving for safe emotional outlets. Kids who aren't rewarded for taking risks. Kids who live on a military base in Okinawa, Japan. When Lisa talks about her work with them, her eyes sparkle and her grin fills the room. She understands her students. Their issues are her issues. She offers them compassion and a radical honesty that they don't get anywhere else. She teases them and defends them and gives them a safe place to stumble around, learning life skills on the way. Right livelihood.

Think of someone you know who is on his or her appropriate path. What are their characteristics? Try listing them on the worksheet at the end of the chapter. Did you list these? Energetic, healthy, happy, filled with joy, empathetic, alive, have a special sense of purpose, visionary, see current reality as an ally, embrace change, inquisitive, committed to seeing reality accurately, connected, don't sacrifice their uniqueness, continuously learning, see their life journey as its own reward, deeply self-confident, acutely aware of their ignorance, ditto for their incompetence, relish their uniqueness, have a sense of humor, humble.

There are others.

The main point is this: People who have the courage to figure out their particular path are happy. Even when the work is excruciatingly difficult. Even if they are fighting a fight (like environmental warriors, for example) that they may never win in their lifetime. It doesn't matter. A match is a match, and appropriate work is like having a constant stream of energy feeding you every day. You don't have time to be bored because there is work to be done. You don't have time to wallow in the unfairness of life because there are mountains to climb. And you don't have time to obsess about the crazymakers in your life because ...you just don't.

So finding your path is highly recommended.

THE AUTHENTIC YOU

Once we have a clear sense of what it feels like to be on an appropriate path, we can start to bring our own values and interests to the surface and analyze them, so we can find our path. And we can give ourselves *permission to plan a successful business or shift a business into something that matches us, to something we can cherish.*

The starting point for the real work ahead is a review of your own life. The worksheet, "An Opportunity to Revisit the Real You," at the end of the chapter offers periods of your life where you can list, with all the honesty you can muster, what you have loved in your life until now. It starts with what you *loved* to do as a kid (before you started to drown in the "shoulds" of your life). How about in your teenage years? What did you *love* to do then? What about those young adult years, say twenty to thirty-five? If you are older than thirty-five, what do you love to do now? In other words, *what do you love so much that you would do it anyway, whether or not you were paid?* There's a business in there somewhere.

If you draw a blank with this exercise, go find photographs of yourself at each of these stages and really look at them. Sitting quietly, you'll remember what you loved. Or ask your family and long-term friends; they will help you to remember as well. When I first did this exercise, I looked at a picture of me at five—I was standing barefoot on a rock, toes curled around it, dressed in bib overalls, braids almost to my waist, a daisy in my hand. Studying the little girl staring back at me, I suddenly remembered that I used to love to ride my bike to the woods near our house and dig a kid-sized pit under the pine trees, fill it with leaves, cover it with branches and then lie in it facing up, staring at the sky for hours. Long hours of silence, staring at one thing...can you see how I was wired for the monastic life?

Or I would bring two or three friends with me and we would spend the day in fantasy, making up stories of conquering new lands and starting our own village in the wild west where girls would rule. No wonder I started my own business and ended up being surrounded by women business owners twenty years later.

The lesson is this. Your life tells you your path if you stop to look at the clues it has been throwing at you all this time.

Once you have given yourself the gift of listing what you love, the next step is to list what you hated in the same time frames. Why? Because most of us don't succeed at the things we have hated, even when we are really skilled at whatever it is. (For example, I excelled at math, even in graduate school. But I hated it. When I tried to make it my life's work in my twenties, I lasted about six months. I was just miserable and so was everyone around me.)

Listing what you hate may cause old wounds to surface. Not to worry. You are much more than your wounds, and besides, even if you don't meditate there are many methods for healing once and for all. This is a good day to start. Plus, all the therapists I know have phones, and many of them are taking new clients.

Here is what I am saying in an excruciatingly long-winded way: Doing something that you hate doing doesn't work. Period. Reason one is that we are miserable when we are spending our days working on something that doesn't feed us emotionally and spiritually. Here is a second reason: If your livelihood depends on something you hate doing, it typically won't get done unless *you pay someone else to do it.* Even though I aced accounting in college, I pay my accountant whatever she tells me to pay her for all the reports and financial planning I need. If you asked me for the financial ratios related to my business or for my monthly cash flow analysis I would refer you to her. I just want to see the results of the analysis, not do the tasks. And to be honest, if I didn't hire this work out, I would still be guessing what my tax payments should be each quarter, after being in business for years.

You'll probably be the same. In the twenty-odd years I've been watching over entrepreneurs' shoulders, this is one trait that appears to be universal. So if you hate math tasks, hire out your bookkeeping. If writing drives you nuts, you'll never write the press releases the media needs to help market your services. Hire them out. Even if you are financially successful, the sheer happiness of doing what you are meant to do is lost to you forever.

WHAT MATTERS TO YOU

While many things matter to all of us, when you are building a business the Buddhist way, focus is critical. In fact, Zen masters teach us that focus is everything. On the worksheet titled, "What Really Matters to You?", your job is threefold. First, please circle the things that really matter to you and cross out the things that just don't matter. If something that is not on the worksheet matters to you, just write it in and circle it.

Then put a star by the five things that matter to you the most, all things considered. (Yes, you can circle six or four. This is not an exact science and one of the most wonderful aspects of adult learning is that we can change exercises to suit us.)

Once you have your starred words, put a box around the top three and shade the boxes in so you can still read them. We'll return to them later. (If this is beginning to feel like an exercise from third grade, I apologize. I've been doing it for years with friends and clients and it always brings to the surface what needs to come up. That's why I put it in the workbook.)

Time to pull together the exercises we've done so far. The *Webster's Dictionary* that sits next to my computer defines values as things or qualities having intrinsic worth. That's the goal—livelihood that has intrinsic worth. Looking at the lists of the things you have loved doing, and the last exercise (the boxes and circles and stars), what are your deepest values? List ten on the "Deepest Values" Sheet. It is also useful to say a few things about each one. Here are some examples from mine:

1. Spiritual growth: because I believe the world is a bit better off when I am my wisest and most compassionate self, and that comes out of spiritual growth.

2. Friendships: because they support and nourish me and protect me from loneliness.

3. Honesty: because it is really important to me to know what I'm really dealing with in any situation.

4. Being in nature: nature and a healthy environment both heal and protect me.

5. A good living (enough money): because it gives me freedom from worrying where I'll live and what I'll eat.

MAKING THE CHOICE

"Discovering our 'reason for being' is one of the toughest challenges that life assigns us. A lot of us go through life on a default setting, not realizing that there are little ways in which we can fine tune the picture of our lives and make it clearer, more colorful, and more meaningful. We all face choices about where we work, how we work, and with whom we work. And not choosing is itself a choice."

Andy Cook, Education Coordinator, Guardian Life Insurance

Once you've zoomed in on values, you can start thinking about the kind of business that best matches them—or look at your existing business through a new lens. In the "Building a Business the Zen Way" workshops, we brainstorm business ideas for everyone, even long-time business owners, until we fill a page for each participant. You could talk a small group of your best friends (family members are OK) through the exercises for this section and ask them to brainstorm with you.

An alternative approach to coming up with business ideas, and one that worked for me, was to make a folder file for myself. I labeled it "Business Ideas" and—for a month—any time I thought of a business idea or read about a business that matched my values and what I love to do, I listed the idea or cut out the information and kept it in the folder.

Then, at the end of the month, I sifted and sorted through all my clippings and two excellent business ideas came right out at me. I then became an investigative reporter and spent another couple of weeks at the public library and on the Internet finding out everything I could about both businesses. That research weeded out one of the ideas as too expensive and risky (a health spa) and verified my idea for a "spiritual Bed and Breakfast" in northern Michigan. I am looking for land now.

Try it out. You will be amazed at how these exercises help you to focus on what really matters to you. At the same time, they'll "give you permission" to let go of ideas that just don't match or won't work. When you get down to one or two serious business ideas, you can work through the rest of the workbook. Or while you are sorting through your many ideas, you can work through the next chapter, "Are You an Entrepreneur?" It will take you through the "homework assignments" that need to be done to prepare you for starting or shoring up a business, whatever type you choose.

While this is not the time to quit whatever work you're doing right now, it is a good time to start paying down any debts you might have just as fast as you can...and to stash some cash if at all possible. Both give you some room to maneuver and take the edge off of the fears of potential homelessness that we all face when we think of going out on our own or expanding what we now have.

IF THIS STARTS TO FEEL PRETTY SCARY

Nobody I know has started or built a business free of fear. The real warriors just move through it. The rest of us find tools to help us work through it. Visualizations of what we want, or of calm environments such as beaches, are one of those tools and can be particularly powerful. To try this out, just sit comfortably in your favorite chair in a quiet room. Quietly breathe in and out until you feel a deep sense of relaxation. I usually pretend that a warm flow of energy is moving from my head to my toes and back again, and by the time it goes back out of my head I am utterly relaxed. Then I start visualizing and continue until I can feel myself calm down.

Susan Jeffers, in *Feel the Fear and Do It Anyway*, offers the following visualization, one that gets rave reviews from many of the people who attend the business training we do at the temple:

In the relaxed state..."I want you to think of a goal that you have in life...a specific goal...and you know that FEAR is keeping you from moving forward toward that goal...

Now what I'd like you to do is imagine yourself approaching that goal 'as if' you had no fear...

I want you to see yourself approaching that goal with a sense of power and confidence in yourself...confidence that it will be all right...

What would you be doing if you had no fear?...

See yourself ... What would you be doing next...if you had no fear?...

Look at the people around you.....How are you relating to them...with no fear?...

How are they relating to you?...

Just enjoy this sense of power and notice your ability to love...and contribute...

And know that this is a feeling always within you...always a part of you...

23

And it is within your capability to move forward in life with that power and that confidence...

See yourself...actualizing your goal...with your power...with your confidence...with your love...and with your contribution...

And slowly ...start to bring yourself back to this room...knowing that that power is available to you...As soon as you begin to act...the power will come forward."

Susan Jeffers, *Feel the Fear and Do It Anyway,* Fawcett Columbine, New York, 1987, p. 207

The same sense of peacefulness and possibilities can surface from chanting for a half hour or more. The chant I use is MAUM, pronounced "ma" as in mama, and "um" as in "um, I'm not sure." You can pick your own tune. Sitting in meditation also helps, as does prayer. Both offer a spaciousness that allows us to sift and sort through fears in a safe place.

RESOURCES

Books That Help

Do What You Are: Discover the Perfect Career for You Through the Secrets of Personality Type, by Paul Tieger and Barbara Barron-Tieger (Little, Brown and Company, $16.95)

Finding Your Perfect Work—the New Career Guide to Making a Living, Creating a Life, by Paul and Sarah Edwards (Putnam, $16.95)

Do What You Love, the Money Will Follow—Discovering Your Right Livelihood, by Marsha Sinetar (Dell Paperback, $11.95)

Zen and the Art of Making a Living—A Practical Guide to Creative Career Design, by Laurence G. Boldt (Penguin, $16.95)

The 1999 What Color Is Your Parachute—A Practical Manual for Job Hunters and Career Changers, by Richard Nelson Bolles (Ten Speed Press, $16.95)

THE CHARACTERISTICS OF SOMEONE WHO IS ON HIS/HER APPROPRIATE PATH

Please list them here. Try to fill the page.

_____

_____

_____

_____

_____

_____

_____

_____

_____

_____

_____

_____

_____

_____

_____

_____

_____

_____

_____

_____

_____

_____

AN OPPORTUNITY TO REVISIT THE REAL YOU: PLEASE LIST WHAT YOU LOVED TO DO IN THESE DIFFERENT TIME PERIODS OF YOUR LIFE:

1. As a kid (up to 12 or 13):

_____

_____

_____

_____

2. As a teen (up to 20 or so):

_____

_____

_____

_____

3. As a young adult (up to 35):

_____

_____

_____

_____

4. As an older adult (after 35):

_____

_____

_____

_____

NOW THINK ABOUT WHAT YOU HATED TO DO AND LIST THOSE THINGS:

1. As a kid (up to 12 or 13):

_____

_____

_____

_____

2. As a teen (up to 20 or so):

_____

_____

_____

_____

3. As a young adult (up to 35):

_____

_____

_____

_____

4. As an older adult (after 35):

_____

_____

_____

_____

WHAT **REALLY** MATTERS TO YOU?

Here's what to do on the next two pages: First circle the things that really matter and cross out those that don't. If something matters to you and isn't on the sheets, just write it in and circle it. Then put a star by the five things that matter the most, all things considered. Once you have your starred words, put a box around the top three and shade the boxes in so you can still read them.

Achievement	Friendships	Challenge
Advancement/Promotion	Growth	Pleasure
Adventure	Having a family	Power
Affection (love and caring)		Helping other people
Arts	Privacy	Public Service
Challenging problems	Honesty	Purity
Change and variety		Independence
Quality of what I take part in		Close relationships
Community	Inner harmony	Recognition

Competence   Integrity   Spirituality

Competition   Intellectual status   Reputation

Job Tranquillity   Responsibility   Creativity

Knowledge   Self Respect   Democracy

Location   Leadership   Serenity

Ecological awareness   Status   Economic security

Loyalty   Sophistication   Stability

Effectiveness   Meaningful work   Efficiency

Merit   Supervising others   Ethics   Nature

Money   Time   Freedom   Excellence

Truth   Excitement   Openness/Honesty of others

Wealth   Expertise   Fame

Order   Work under pressure   Work alone

Considering all the exercises you've done so far:

WHAT ARE YOUR DEEPEST VALUES?

1. _____

_____

2. _____

_____

3. _____

_____

4. _____

_____

5. _____

_____

6. _____

_____

7. _____

_____

8. _____

_____

9. _____

_____

10. _____

_____

RIGHT LIVELIHOOD CHOICES
THAT COULD MATCH MY VALUES:

1. _____

_____

_____

_____

2. _____

_____

_____

_____

3. _____

_____

_____

_____

4. _____

_____

_____

_____

5. _____

_____

_____

_____

KARMIC JACKPOT:
THE #1 BUSINESS IDEA

After a month (or at least several weeks), please answer this question for yourself:

> What is my favorite business idea, the one I would do without pay?
>
> List it here:

_____

_____

_____

_____

_____

_____

(It's OK to have one or two or even three at this point. They'll shake out as you go through the rest of the workbook. On the other hand, if you don't have an answer, it is probably a good idea to stay with this chapter for awhile...until something surfaces.)

Chapter Three

Are You an Entrepreneur?

Travis is a hunk. Braids, body, grin. I can only imagine his reaction when he first came to the Community Development Corporation's business training and realized he was about to spend four intensive weeks with a bunch of women old enough to be his mother. To his credit he hung in there with us, braving discussions of perimenopause and children and country & western singers. An artiste to the bone, Travis is a brilliant graffiti artist. For several years he couldn't make a connection between his art and making any money, let alone a right livelihood business—until he moved to Gainesville, Florida. There he discovered etching and transformed his talent into a mobile "etching" business where he puts up a booth at car shows and etches logos, names, and personalized graffiti art onto the owners' vehicles. Here's the right livelihood part: his customers keep their vehicles longer and, I think Travis would argue, they take better care of their cars or trucks since they are no longer modes of transportation but traveling art.

The amazing thing about Travis is that he works the night shift at UPS so he can use his days to build his business and take care of his three-year-old. An entrepreneur's entrepreneur, he started taking himself seriously when he couldn't find a job in Michigan after moving north from Florida. Given the size of the market, and his growth curve, he will be a millionaire in about seven years.

MAKING THE TRANSITION: SIX MILESTONES

When you decide it's time to move into serious "building a business" mode, you'll find that all the parts of your life may need revisiting. In the Ann Arbor sangha (community), we are constantly chanting the phrase, "impermanence surrounds us." This is a truth that becomes magnified when businesses are developed. Things change. Things need to change. And homework needs to be done.

The transition from where you are right now to a deeper embracing of right livelihood calls for some real soul searching, not that you need to believe in a soul to do the search. Deep questions need responses. Who is the company you keep? Are they a match for you, the business owner? What is your vision of the life you want to lead? What will serve as a royal kick in the butt to get you started? Radical honesty is critical.

The Company You Keep

Having said all this, there are risk takers in life and there are people who just don't even want to think about it. Most of us surround ourselves with risk-averse people...for good reasons. They are dependable, stick with us, stick up for us, drive cars that don't fall apart on highways. This is a problem, however, when we decide that we want to start our own businesses, or grow one we already have. Here's why. When we decide that we want to go out into the great unknown as a business owner or to significantly shift an existing business, it can strike terror into the hearts of all who are dear to us. And to demonstrate their great devotion to us they will list all of the reasons why we should stay put. Over and over. Because they love us. And starting or building a business is risky.

The only trouble with their reactions is that we need to be able to take risks if our lives are going to change in any significant way. So we need to meet and spend time with other entrepreneurs, people who have leapt into the great unknown before us...and lived to tell about it. People who are already building right livelihood businesses can be wonderfully helpful to emerging owners. They are proof that right livelihood is possible. They teach us the passes through the mountains of barriers. They give us advice we can use.

Keep company with these people. Find them at church, at the temple, at health food stores, holistic health centers, on the net. And spend time with them. Learn their stories. Ask about the mistakes. Doing this will fast-forward your learning curve. Plus, you will end up with a new set of interesting, positive, spirituality driven, and earthy friends.

Decide Your Own Values and Vision

We've covered values. Now it is time for visioning. A vision statement is a description of your preferred future state, the life you want to live, and the company you want to create. In a way it is our deepest statement of what we really want. It reflects our core values and helps us to focus on what we need to do. What is the future that you want? On the worksheet, "Personal Vision," describe your life ten years from now. What are you doing? Where are you living? What is the community like? How big is the business? What are your offices like? What technology are you using? What are you selling? How are you selling it? Are there employees? What is your income?

It is impossible to be too specific. Each year on January 1, I actually make a collage of what I hope for that year. Everything is on it: income, activities, people, places, the products I want to offer, vacations. And then I try not to be too amazed as I check off each of the things as they happen! I've gotten so that I think twice before I put anything onto the collage, to double check that I really want whatever it is to take place. That's how sure I am that it will happen. (Even though I am often unclear about *how* it will happen.)

Making the Decision to Do It

Nothing happens until we decide to do it. Ever.

---

*"Whatever you can do or dream you can, begin
it. Boldness has genius, magic, and power in it.
Begin it now."* —*Goethe*

You need to decide that you deserve the life that you want; to make
your living in a way that is consistent with your values. Make yourself 1)
a promise to start; and 2) a deadline. Write the deadline down and get
someone to witness it for you. Put it on your refrigerator and plan a party
for yourself to celebrate when you follow through. And it will happen. To
facilitate this exercise, there is a "Vow" form at the back of this chapter.
Find a witness, make the vow, and then hang it somewhere where you'll
see it all the time. Like the back of your front door.

Stashing Cash

I will only admit it this one time: You can start a business without any
cash, but it is incredibly hard. When I was first working with people
who were starting their businesses, the rule of thumb was that you
needed a year's worth of cash stashed to be "safe" while the emerging
business took shape or an existing business shifted to a new line or
lines. These days it takes longer for most businesses to kick in ...more
like a year and a half. In other words, it takes most businesses between
a year and a year and a half to break even or pay for themselves. As a
result, most of us need subsidies. They can come in the form of savings
accounts or money market accounts we can draw on, second mortgages on a house (my favorite) if you are lucky enough to be a home-
owner, or a line of credit, usually in the form of several VISA cards, that
you can use to pay bills.

If risk is as scary to you as the other 99 percent of society, you might
want to figure out how you can work part-time or at a job that doesn't
require a lot of hard thinking (so you can use your brain cells on the
building of your business), while you build your company on the side.

That's what Travis did. In fact, as I think about it, as many as half of all the people who have gone through "Building a Business the Zen Way" training have started their businesses this way.

Only *you* know how much risk you can stand. Be honest and plan accordingly. For right livelihood businesses, *I do not recommend* venture capital, private investors other than family, or even bank loans, unless you are more than sure that you can pay them back in a timely manner. The reason? Because each of these forms of financing can put enormous pressure on a business to grow faster than its natural growth curve. I've watched too many business owners compromise their own values over the years because they have been under so much pressure to make money for their investors and/or stockholders. So be careful.

Resolving Outstanding Life Issues

It takes concentration and focus to build a business of integrity. Both are difficult if you have other outstanding life issues in your face. See if you can come clean before you start. If you are a practicing alcoholic or drug user, it's time to head for help. If you have any closets to come out of, it's time to come out. I had to write a final, "You are the meanest son of a bitch on earth and I forgive you but I won't forget," letter to my father before I could concentrate on my own business. If you have amends to make, make them. Want a baby? Have it now before you start in on building the business. Time to get married or unmarried? Do it now.

It is better to postpone the start-up or a growth phase for a business than to try to take on too much. Your divided attention and distractions weaken your own efforts to pull the entity together. And frankly, I have yet to see an entrepreneur make a wise decision when he or she is truly distracted by other significant emotional issues.

Taking the First Step

Here's what I had to do: When I decided that it was time to start my own business, I was making a ton of money (for me anyway) as a management consultant. And every time I said to myself, "OK, self, THIS IS THE YEAR you quit," I would get a great raise or bonus or both. Plus, I had lots of excellent excuses to stay in employee mode—like health benefits, a mortgage payment, a daughter who needed braces. Still, I knew in my heart of hearts that I really wanted to be on my own, doing right livelihood.

Finally, I picked a date, and I asked my best friends to come to my office and literally pick me up and carry me out the door if I hadn't resigned by then. Frankly, the sheer terror that they would follow through with great aplomb was enough to make me give notice and leave on my own. So decide what your first step is, and then make it public. Tell everyone who will listen. Write it on your bathroom mirror. Set yourself up so there are negative consequences for not following through (like your friends making fun of you for the rest of your life), and you'll take the first step.

A SELF-ASSESSMENT

How can you tell when you're really "ready" to go into business or shift to the next level in your existing business? When I first started reading about successful entrepreneurs and then getting to know them, I noticed that they had certain characteristics. Before reviewing them, a useful pre-exercise is to go through this chapter's Self-Assessment Worksheet on your own. It will give you a pretty sound reading of how ready you are to start a right livelihood business or expand what you have. When you are finished, the section below explains the themes that make up the questions.

What the Self-Assessment Means

1. Long hours and little sleep. The business owners I know work around sixty hours a week, at least in the first three years or so. I still struggle to keep my week to forty hours (even though I'm a lot better off than my sixty to eighty hours of six years ago). For most people, emerging businesses or shifts in existing businesses are started as an additional daily activity until they kick in and prove they'll feed you and yours. What that means is that the extra time you'll need could come out of your sleeping hours. Just so you are warned.

2. Tolerating uncertainty. Impermanence surrounds us. One of the sure truths of our lives is that nothing is certain. In any business, *nothing is certain.* You never know for sure if you will have customers, even if your business is earth- and people-friendly. Maybe you'll be too hard to find. You never know for sure what customers will buy, even when they do find you. Or when they will pay. Or even how they'll pay. Uncertainty is one of those costs of business ownership. It helps to remind yourself that since nothing in life is certain anyway, you might as well own your own business. At least you'll be doing something that matches your values and is consistent with the precepts.

3. Risk taking. Taking risks means making decisions and taking actions without knowing the result. This is courage. To be risk takers, we each need to be ready to change if we need to, to look foolish occasionally, to be uncomfortable. People who build right livelihood businesses take risks every day, not the least of which is making their values public. They take risks deciding which services they'll market. The bank they'll use. The people they choose as teammates.

The most successful risk takers simply make the decision, or do the action, and just keep moving forward without obsessing too much about the potential downside of what they just did.

" When we line up all the facts we think are against us, the facts can stop us before we start. Whatever we need to discourage us—I'm too young, too old, too short, too tall, unprepared, inexperienced or not quite ready—we can uncover. And if we miss a few details, we can always find someone to help us 'face the facts.' The facts after all speak for themselves—except they're not true. Courage is doing it anyway, whatever it is. We all doubt ourselves ....we all wonder whether we really have the goods."

—Marlo Thomas

---

4.   *High self-confidence.* Since you'll need it, it's a good thing you have it. If you are unsure, dig into your spiritual practice, whatever it is. It will remind you. Success happens to people who believe in themselves and in their ability to figure out what needs to be done in a specific situation. In a recent American Express survey of successful business owners, 82 percent estimated their chance of survival at 9 out of 10 at the start of the business. Now *that* is self-confidence.

When people go to him for advice about risky situations, my teacher Sunim is always saying this: In any difficult situation, you have three tasks: 1. Don't panic (because panic doesn't help anything). 2. Assess the situation. In other words, we need to truly understand what is going on in a given situation. 3. Do the obvious. Doing the obvious assumes self-confidence—that we trust ourselves to do what's best or at a minimum what's "good enough" in any situation.

5.   *Persistence.* Your mother probably called it stubbornness. Persistence is the ability to just keep going. It is the absence of sloth and half-heartedness. This quality is highly recommended for people building a business the Buddhist way. Promise yourself to stay with this for *as long as it takes. Think in terms of years.*

6.   *Goals and objectives.* To succeed in business, it takes an ability to set, and then meet, goals and objectives. In other words, you will need to create tangible measures of success for yourself so you can tell how you are doing. What is it that you really want to accomplish? Is it a business that can support a particular number of employees? How earth-friendly can you be? Do you want to create a new industry? Do you simply want to sell four strategic planning projects each year so you can pay for living expenses and volunteer in an urban school system?

What is it? Write it down. Goals and objectives also deserve refrigerator space.

7.   *Obstacles* are everywhere. They start when close friends and family members tell you they are concerned about you, or if you are like me, that you are going to hell. (I never did figure out that connection.) Obstacles may show up in the form of bankers who won't loan you start-up funds, or employees who all decide to quit on the same day. (This just happened at my favorite coffee shop. How will we live without our double lattes?!) You could make a commitment to develop a truly family-friendly television show in six months and discover that you have hepatitis on the same day.

Obstacles are grist for your evolving mill. Best strategy? Face them head on. Define them, figure out their scale, and then strategize how you are going to get around them. Think like water. Instead of fighting the obstacles, look for ways around them and for the cracks where you can seep through them. After awhile you'll realize that obstacles can actually be entertaining, and appreciate them for their ability to keep you from ever being bored.

8. Failure. There isn't any such thing. This whole drill we call life is about one thing: evolving spiritually. When things don't go as planned, they simply haven't gone as planned. There are probably a bundle of lessons in the experience, but failure? None. Failure is an illusion, thought up by somebody who wanted to brag about creating a word. Don't even waste a breath thinking about it. Things don't work out? Refocus. Bring in your most creative friends and wisest teacher and work out a different means to your entrepreneurial end.

9. Asking for help. Every day I take refuge in Buddha, dharma (the teachings of the Buddha), and sangha (the community of all of us). Each is a reminder that none of us is alone and that asking for help is part of creating a right livelihood life. Nobody does this stuff alone. Nobody.

10. Responsibility for your decisions. OK, I admit it. There are days when I really wished I had a boss who I could blame for all the problems in my life. As a business owner, you can't blame anyone else for the decisions you make. Ever. When things go wrong, our tendency is to look around for a scapegoat—for someone or something to blame—an "if only." If only the client had made her decisions earlier, I could have made the deadlines. If only the bank had given me a larger credit line, I wouldn't be bankrupt.

Unfortunately there are no scapegoats for right livelihood entrepreneurs. All your decisions need to be your own. It is a waste of time and precious energy to look for someone else to blame if you make an unwise decision. You don't have that time and energy to spare. I say take the hit and keep going. Denying and abandoning your personal responsibility for *all aspects of the business* is like throwing oil on a tiny flame—it can make minor problems explosive.

11. Total immersion. When I was in the Maitreya Buddhist Seminary, one of my teacher's constant teachings was "dig one well." He was telling us that if we get too distracted doing too many things, we won't master any of them. To build your business, you need to allow the business to take on a primary role in your life, for awhile anyway. It needs your best energy in the same way a child does. No other business distractions. This is the one that has won your heart.

12. Ethics. They matter. When you are building a right livelihood business you have a head start because its roots are ethical. Even so, it is important to remind yourself not to get swept away by the diseases of the ego like greed, misrepresentation, flippancy, and the need to find and use scapegoats. In the end, all you have is your personal behavior to keep you safe. Money won't help.

13. Taking charge. There is something utterly freeing about building your own business. You are the one in charge. You are the one making the most important decisions. And you are the one who sets the direction, rhythm, and pace of the business.

FACING DRAGONS

Dragons are our fears. They are the biggest obstacles that any business owner faces, and everyone has them. The best way to deal with dragons is to first name them. Often when this has been done, they disappear of their own accord because the wise part of you realizes that they are unfounded. Or, as the Dalai Lama teaches, there is no point in worrying about something. Either you can do something about it or you can't. If you can do something, do it. Otherwise just move on.

When I was starting my business, one of my mountain-sized dragons was my fear that my daughter and I would somehow end up homeless and starve to death. When I wrote it down on a sheet similar to the "Facing Dragons" page in this workbook, I just grinned. Even when I was a graduate student with no real income and no outside financial support, I had been able to figure out ways to make ends meet. Several part-time jobs at a time. House sharing. The point is that I've never starved and we've always had a roof over our heads. So the dragon was vaporware. Realizing this truth has helped me to stare down every dragon that has surfaced since then.

If your own dragons don't go away, then your job is to come up with ways to deal with them and then build those ways into your business strategies. If you are afraid you won't have enough money to hire staff, start with subcontractors—or barter. If you are afraid the product or service won't sell, do a mini sales campaign to get consumer feedback before you invest too much into supplies. And if you can't come up with ideas, try the visualization exercise in the previous chapter. If that doesn't work, I suggest you find a professional business counselor, or even a therapist, to help you work through your anxiety. Ask other entrepreneurs what they did when they faced similar fears. Read magazines and newspapers, and investigate entrepreneurial chat rooms on the Internet. Join associations related to your industry. Track down your local Chamber of Commerce and Small Business Administration staff to see what they offer. While it is true that we are each unique, it is also true that the fears related to starting and building a business are, sorry to say, fairly commonplace. I've never found a dragon who couldn't be faced, and ultimately stared down.

PERSONAL VISION: TEN YEARS OUT

What do you want your life to be like ten years from now? Things to consider: place, what you'll be doing, what the business will be, housing, the people who will be in your life.

This exercise is best done as stream-of-consciousness writing. In other words, just start and keep writing until you have written enough to create a vivid picture in the mind of someone else who is reading your words. When I do this exercise, every time I start to slow down I just ask myself, "What else?" Only when I ask myself, "What else?" and no thoughts surface do I let myself put down my pen.

_____

_____

_____

_____

_____

_____

_____

_____

_____

_____

_____

_____

_____

_____

_____

_____

_____

_____
_____
_____
_____
_____
_____
_____
_____
_____
_____
_____
_____
_____
_____
_____
_____
_____
_____
_____
_____
_____
_____
_____
_____
_____
_____

A SELF-ASSESSMENT

(Hopefully you'll answer yes to all of these.)

1. Can you work long hours with little sleep for the first year(s) if you need to?

   _____

2. Can you tolerate uncertainty?

   _____

3. Do you take risks?

   _____

4. Do you enjoy taking risks?

   _____

5. Do you have high self-confidence?

   _____

6. Are you persistent?

   _____

7. Do you know how to set goals and objectives for yourself?

   _____

8. Can you meet those goals and objectives?

   _____

9. Do you enjoy facing obstacles to see what it will take to get past them?

   _____

10. Do you know how to use failure as a learning experience?

_____

11. Do you ask for help and advice when you need it?

_____

12. Can you accept responsibility for important decisions?

_____

13. Do you have the ability to become totally immersed in the building of a business?

_____

14. Are you always ethical?

_____

15. Are you able to take charge?

_____

16. Are you always reliable? (In other words, do you do what you say you'll do when you say you'll do it?)

_____

17. Do you always deal honestly with other people?

_____

THE OFFICIAL BUILDING A BUSINESS THE BUDDHIST WAY VOW

_____
Date

I will start: _____
(describe the company)

or build: _____
(describe the company)

to _____
(what level of sales)

by _____
(deadline)

_____
(your name)

_____
(witness)

OFFICIAL SEAL
OF APPROVAL

FACING DRAGONS

All of the obstacles I am facing	Solutions to the obstacles

Do or not do. There is no try.

—Yoda

Chapter Four

The Business Plan

Some say the road to hell is paved with good intentions. When you are trying to build a business of integrity, one that honors the earth, the same sort of truth holds. Good intentions do not a success make. Your path to a thriving business needs to be paved with a well-thought-out business plan followed by actions based on that plan. I once read somewhere that 80 percent of all businesses fail. My guess is that they did not have plans because the ones that do seem to succeed. For entrepreneurs building a business the Buddhist way, a business plan is your fourth refuge, after Buddha, Dharma, and Sangha. It protects you and your vision from many of the hazards that could otherwise cut you off at the knees.

So what is a business plan? More than anything else, a business plan is a *strategy document.* It defines who your company is, what business you are in, the goals you have for yourself and your business, and how you plan to accomplish those goals. As such it is an invaluable dry run because it forces you (and it is the *only thing that does*) to take an objective, critical, and (hopefully) unemotional look at your possible future.

For these reasons alone, a business plan is important. It also matters because it is a sales document of sorts, selling your vision for your company to several audiences that you need on your side to succeed. The first is your internal audience. It has one member—you. Every entrepreneur who has taken the time to write a business plan before she starts or expands a business will tell you that most of the anxieties—and sometimes all of them—related to making decisions around the business dissipate when they write a plan. That's because it has facilitated facing their dragons and forced them to make the key decisions they need to make to move the company forward. Think of a business plan as preventative medicine in this regard. And while I'm on this soapbox, let me add that if your plan doesn't convince you of the merit of your own business, then it is not the business for you.

The second audience is made up of anyone who is a stakeholder in your business, where stakeholder means someone who can be impacted by your decisions. Your emotional partner. Your father if he is living with you. Spouses. Kids. Pets. Best friends. Also employees if you have them or will be hiring them.

External audiences also matter here. First in line is your banker or other investors. If you insist on raising money from someone else, then a business plan is a given. Service professionals, including your accountant (who will teach you the rules of the Internal Revenue Service), attorney, and insurance agent, also need to see your plan. Why? Because they have a role in helping you to get from here to there by introducing you to potential clients and other business owners who could be very supportive of your plans. I even share business plans with key suppliers.

THE PARTS OF A PLAN

First let me say this. A business plan does not have to be a fancy document to be a good business plan. What matters is that it is thorough, addressing the key aspects of your enterprise. It also does not need to be long. These days a business plan longer than 10 pages makes me incredibly nervous. Why? Because you want to be able to find sections quickly, and refer to them often. User friendliness matters. I stopped writing full paragraphs years ago and use bullets and graphs wherever possible. Efficient communication is your goal.

Every business plan needs a cover page that tells the reader the name of the company, its key contact person (that's you), address, phone number, fax, and email address. This page also needs a statement that declares the document as confidential and, for the truly paranoid, a number. (In other words, you only want to print a limited number of business plans that you track closely, numbering each one in one of the bottom corners of the cover page.)

The Executive Summary

As for the plan itself, there are three parts: the executive summary, the body of the plan, and the financial section. The executive summary is short, one to three pages. It contains the key information about your business that you would want people to read, knowing that you only have about a minute's worth of their attention. A good summary names the business, lists products, and explains why the business is this business instead of anything else. It covers values, key milestones such as when you started it, when you introduced your first products (or when you will), how large you expect the company to grow, and who the key players are. If you are writing the plan to raise money, you'll need to mention that in the executive summary as well.

The Body

The body of the plan is really the key section because it tells your story. So put in all the information you need to, until an unrelated reader can describe your business back to you. Basically the body of the plan covers six core topics:

- company description,
- your products,
- management,
- your marketing plan,
- an action plan, and
- a risk analysis.

There are no rules that I know of regarding the actual order of these topics. My vote is that you start with a description of the company and services—to set the stage—and then do the other sections in the order that makes the most sense to you.

Company Description: This section, which is typically two or three pages *at the most* , includes your vision for the company, what the business is all about, your core objectives, and how you plan to run it. It talks about expected milestones and tells the reader the form of the business— whether you are incorporated, a limited liability company, a sole proprietor, etc. (If you are unclear about what form of business makes the most sense in your situation, get advice from your accountant. Because the form depends on your lifestyle, personal assets, and type of business, there is no generic way to determine the form or structure of the business that will work best for you.)

This first section is where you set your goals and objectives for the company. If you have been in business for awhile, you can also describe your history. Be sure to say specifically why you think your business will succeed.

The Products: Next comes a description of your products or services. It is worth the trouble to describe each one in detail to see if there are any missing pieces (such as how you'll provide customer service related to your products after they are sold.)

Then, keeping in mind the precepts, describe both the strengths *and* weaknesses of your offerings, relative to your competition. The strengths will be easy; the weaknesses will be painful. You'll need to discuss what you can do to rid yourself of the weaknesses…to make them go away. If you don't, your business will have a terrible time trying to grow because it will be swimming upstream. Here is an example. Let's say that one of your product weaknesses is that you totally rely on one supplier of hemp for your perma-grocery-bag line. You'll need to neutralize it by finding other suppliers you can depend on in case your product line takes off much faster than you expected.

Management: Typically, management comes next. The key part of this section consists of a description of the actual number and types of positions you have now, and the ones you are planning to create. Include the functions that you are planning to subcontract out. Each position, including subcontractor or part-time positions, then needs a job description. Writing out people's responsibilities and authority is an exercise that will save you time, money, and possible lawsuits later.

Here's how I write this section: First I draw an organizational chart that depicts the company the way it will be when it is "all grown-up" (or at least a couple of years out), with a box for each staff person. In one of the corners of each box I've drawn for a staff person, I write in the year when the person will be joining the company. Then I use the rest of the box for a summary of the person's job description, written in bullet form. If I already know the name of the person filling the position, I write her name on the top line inside the appropriate box.

Under the box? Several lines that explain to the reader (and that will remind you, on the chance that you end up lying awake at night wondering why you picked a particular person for this task) why the person named is the right person for the job. If what I am saying here simply doesn't make sense, take a look at the worksheet page labeled "The Body/Management."

The Market: The marketing section of a business plan is really a mini marketing plan in disguise. If you already have a marketing plan, you simply insert it here. Your main goal in this section is to convince the reader that you really have a market, i.e., customers who want and will buy your products or services, and that you know how to get their attention.

Most marketing sections start with an environmental analysis. This is simply a description of the world around you—the economy, politics, technological trends, and demographic trends—and how those factors are likely to impact what you are trying to do. A more in-depth description of this section can be found in the marketing section of the workbook.

One of the most painful moments of truth in building a business comes when you think about customers. Who are they *really*? You must describe them in excruciating detail. You must know them intimately (within the parameters of the precepts!). *This is the most important section of your plan* and has two parts. The first is a profile of the specific characteristics of your PERFECT CUSTOMER. It includes the age of the person, sex, income, education, family situation, likes and dislikes, buying behavior (for example, will he or she buy over the Internet?), lifestyle, church affiliation, location, and any other information that helps you to separate the people who will happily buy from you from those who won't buy anything from you, ever. If your customers are working for companies that you are selling to as well (as opposed to selling to individuals directly), then you also need to profile the type of company that employs them. Similar characteristics work. What is the age of the company? Its size in terms of revenues? Number of employees? How are decisions made? Is it hierarchical? Where are headquarters located? What industry is it in? Is it an industry you want to sell to?

Again, in my experience it is impossible to list too many characteristics for your profiles. The more you know about who you are selling to, the less you will waste in marketing—as measured by time, energy, expense, and trees harvested for paper. You won't contact people who just are not going to buy from you, or send materials to the wrong person. This approach eliminates all sorts of inefficiencies.

Once the target clients are profiled, the follow-up task is to estimate how many of them exist. You need a big enough market to be able to sell to the market and make a living. In the best situations the market is big enough to support you *and* your competitors *and* your growth. This is a research process that is critical. If you can't find any existing data about the market you want to sell to, talk to potential clients yourself to see if you are on the right path. They'll tell you.

Competition will surface as you do the client research. We all have it. The way to think about competition is to ask yourself who (or what) is doing what you want to do right now. Think "out of the box." For me, for example, while there may not be another training program that directly teaches people about right livelihood businesses, there are books and workbooks that can teach budding entrepreneurs as much as I can. And they stay put so you can find them when you want them, compared to my always-on-the-move lifestyle. So they *are* competition for "Building a

Business the Zen Way" workshops, as are other entrepreneurs who are willing to coach people through the building of a business.

An important exercise is to ask your most honest friends who your competition will be. If they don't know, ask other entrepreneurs or those potential clients you just described. They will know. Then summarize what they tell you in your plan. What do they like about the competition? What are the strengths of their products? How about the downside? What don't they like? What do you need to do to compete with the strengths of the competition? This may include your packaging, what you do exactly, how you get people's attention, how you sell, and your customer service. There any many, many possibilities here.

Your business has to have unique qualities, or your customers won't be able to single you out in the crowd. The more things that are unique— as long as you are still providing the benefits that your customers want— the better off you will probably be. This uniqueness is your *market position*. Once you figure out what it is, you'll need to stick with it, and market it (i.e., your uniqueness) as much as the actual products or services you are selling.

All of your thoughts about these market-related themes need to be summarized in the business plan in the form of sales and marketing objectives. Pricing policies and the customer service you will provide also need to surface somewhere in here. All the different ways you will promote your product need to be listed and described as well. A forewarning: Be careful not to get carried away. I always think I can do significantly more marketing than I can ever afford. It's that optimistic gene we business owners were born with. Yours will probably kick in right about here too.

At the end of the market section of the plan it is helpful to summarize the expected results of all of your marketing and sales activities. For example, you may expect special events to draw thirty people per event to your organic juice bar, or if you advertise your writing seminar six times in your local paper twenty people will register at $80 per person.

The Action Plan: Last lap. If you are actually building a product, this is where you describe your manufacturing process—preferably with pictures. You'll need a step-by-step description of the process, including *where* you'll make the product, as well as a listing of suppliers, what each will be providing, and in what quantities. It is also a good idea to include a typical production schedule in the plan, to prove to yourself that the timelines you have in your head will really work. A critical issue related to manufacturing is your back-up plan for *each step of the manufacturing process.* That needs to be figured out and described in this section as well.

Even if you aren't making a product, but are providing a service, it is worthwhile to make a sketch of the process you'll use to design, implement, and deliver what you sell. My business plan includes about ten steps for my strategic planning process modules. I summarize each step, including who needs to do what tasks, as well as the time needed and expenses expected to accrue. This exercise forces me to clarify exactly how I am going to pull off what I've promised. It also gives me something to look at whenever I feel like I'm getting off track, reminding me where I'm headed and what tasks still need finishing for the project to be successful.

The rest of your action plan pulls the business plan together in the form of a monthly chart that summarizes all the tasks and responsibilities of the business. As is true with the marketing section, the more detail, the better. Down a column on the left side of a page, list all the major chores that need to be done over the course of a year. Across the top of the page, list all of the months of the year. Then you can make a checkmark in the month when each task needs to be accomplished and add the initials of the person responsible for doing each chore. (Look at the worksheet called "The Action Plan" to see what I am trying desperately to describe here.) When you fill in the chart you have just created, task by task, you are creating an invaluable summary of the entire plan. I actually try to make a chart for each of the next three years (even if I'm only writing a one-year business plan) so I have some idea of what is ahead of me with the business.

An alternative action plan is offered below:

Action Plan 2001

For the fiscal year 2001, Jamison's Jumping Jacks is concentrating on the completion of its product line and the start-up of sales. The company is also networking several functions, including inventory, sales, and its financial tracking system.

Milestones:	Completed By:
Completion of product lines	4/30/01
Networking system for inventory in place	5/31/01
Hiring sales staff	6/30/01
Networking system for financial management system in place	6/30/01
Policy manuals/staff policies updated by executive team	10/31/01
Sales training program implemented	12/31/01

Contingency Plan: I remember working with an investor who had only one rule about success: He used to say that entrepreneurs who did not think through potential crises were doomed to failure. In deference to his wisdom, the last section of the body of your plan, called the contingency plan (or risk analysis), offers an opportunity to think about things that could go wrong. This is where you list them. You also need to figure out potential solutions to any potential risks you think up and list those as well. Without potential solutions the business will be at a real disadvantage, relative to its competition. Frankly, I would rethink the entire business if I had a risk I couldn't address.

The Financial Section

Once you've written the body of the plan, the hardest work is done. Next step? Get your accountant to translate your story into numbers. A trick that will help her, and that will save you money later because she won't have to figure out what you were thinking when you wrote the plan, is to keep a running tab of any assumptions you make related to money (making it and spending it) as you write the various sections. Here are some of the kinds of assumptions you'll make: what you'll pay subcontractors, when sales will come in, how people will pay, when service providers will bill you. Listing them on a sheet of paper that you've labeled "Assumption Page" as you think of them will save you hours and hours of time later when you find yourself trying to reconstruct what the heck you were thinking when you wrote each of the sections of the plan.

The accountant will translate the numbers into a cash flow, or yearly budget, that you will be able to use to track your progress. Since there are a number of good software programs out there that track cash flow, you might want to ask the accountant to set up a system for you to use to input financial data yourself. Then he can just look over your shoulder on a regular basis to make sure you are doing OK. Once the financial section is complete, you are ready to kick into gear.

CRIB SHEETS FOR THE BUSINESS PLAN CHAPTER

1. What is a business plan?

    _____

    _____

    _____

    _____

    _____

2. Why is it important?

    _____

    _____

    _____

    _____

    _____

    _____

THE PARTS OF A BUSINESS PLAN

A. The Executive Summary

B. The Body of the Plan

C. The Financial Section

    1. The Assumption Page

    2. Cash Flow Projections (for the life of the plan)

    3. The Balance Sheet (This is only necessary if you have assets and are going after financing. See the finance chapter if none of this is making sense.)

A FORMAT FOR YOUR COVER SHEET

Business Plan

Your Company Name

Your Company Address

Contact Person

Phone / fax / e-mail address

A confidentiality statement goes here—something that says that the only people who can see this document are the people you give the plan to.

_____

Plan #   Date

A SUGGESTED FORMAT
FOR THE BODY OF THE PLAN

A. The Company

1) Your story: history, values, objectives, milestones, etc.

2) Products or services

Product Description	Strengths	Potential Problems	Solutions to Potential Problems
Product #1:			
Product #2:			
Product #3:			

(Just keep adding all your products and services so you can describe them, their strengths, potential problems, and your solutions to the problems)

B. Management and Personnel

For each person in the company, write a description that includes title, all responsibilities, number of hours per week, wages, technology available to him/her. See the sample organizational chart on the next page, or simply list all your staff and describe their roles this way:

Title:
_____

Responsibilities:
_____

_____

_____

Hours per week:
_____

Wage:
_____

Benefits:
_____

Technology available to perform duties:
_____

_____

_____

(If there are a lot of people who do the same job, such as customer relations staff, you can just write one description and then indicate how many people are responsible for the function. I also include descriptions of board members, all contract and part-time employees, and my service professionals—attorney, accountant, and banker.)

Title:

Responsibilities:

Hours per week:

Wages:

Benefits:

Technology:

Skill Summary: _____

_____

Title:

Responsibilities:

Hours per week:

Wages:

Benefits:

Technology:

Skill Summary: _____

_____

Title:

Responsibilities:

Hours per week:

Wages:

Benefits:

Technology:

Skill Summary: _____

_____

Title:

Responsibilities:

Hours per week:

Wages:

Benefits:

Technology:

Skill Summary: _____

_____

Title:

Responsibilities:

Hours per week:

Wages:

Benefits:

Technology:

Skill Summary: _____

_____

Title:

Responsibilities:

Hours per week:

Wages:

Benefits:

Technology:

Skill Summary: _____

_____

Title:

Responsibilities:

Hours per week:

Wages:

Benefits:

Technology:

Skill Summary: _____

_____

C. The Market

1) Context: (What is going on in the world outside of your business that is going to impact you one way or the other? See the marketing section for more details on this.)

_____

_____

_____

_____

_____

_____

_____

_____

_____

_____

2) Customers:

a. A profile of your perfect customer goes here.

_____

_____

_____

_____

_____

_____

_____

_____

_____

_____

b. Estimates of how many of those people or companies exist go here. _____

3) Competition

Competitor	His / her strengths	Weaknesses	How you can neu- tralize the strengths
Competitor #1			
Competitor #2			
Competitor #3			

(include name, address, phone)

(You could have as many as seven. More than that? Rethink your market. It's too many.)

4) Market position

_____

_____

_____

_____

_____

_____

_____

_____

_____

_____

5) Market plan (This is basically a task and timeline of all the things
    you'll do to get the attention of your customers.)

_____

_____

_____

_____

_____

_____

_____

_____

_____

_____

D. The Manufacturing Process (or process for implementing the services you provide)

_____

_____

_____

_____

_____

_____

Draw a picture of your manufacturing process here.

E. The Action Plan

Action Steps	Month 1	Month 2	Month . . .	Month 12
Step #1				
Step #2				
Step #3				

There will be many steps. I usually have about twenty for my annual business plan. Some are marketing tasks, some are operational, and some are financial.

F. Risk Analysis

Potential Risks	Potential Solutions

G. The Financials (See your accountant for these unless you have a passion for numbers.)

ASSUMPTION PAGE

(This is the page you take to your accountant, so she can crunch your numbers into a cash-flow budget for you to live by.)

Chapter Five

Marketing Basics

Psychotherapy is right livelihood. As I understand it, therapy is about facilitating sanity—clearing out neuroses, pushing through the mountains of distortions that drive our days. Every time we do a "Building a Business the Zen Way" workshop at the temple, two or three therapists are in the room. I can always spot them because they are the most skilled listeners. They also tend to take copious notes and offer immediately usable feedback to other participants, especially when we talk about facing dragons. On the other hand, marketing is not one of their strong suits. I have yet to meet a therapist who has had the benefit of significant training in marketing. As a result, most tell me that everyone needs their particular services. While that may be true, everyone *won't* be a client, and trying to get in front of too many potential clients can drive a therapist's budget into the ground in the time it takes me to type this chapter. (About a week. I'm slow.) Marketing can get incredibly expensive. Quickly. What the therapists learn by putting up with my unasked-for opinions on every topic in the world today is that each has a very specific market made up of potential clients who play to the personal strengths of the therapist, appreciate their style, are nearby, show up for sessions, and pay their bills.

When these therapists identify their real customer base through market research, their clients rarely overlap. Better yet, they are then able to develop and implement efficient and effective marketing campaigns that get the attention of the people they can best help.

Cindy is a tall, soft-spoken, bespectacled MSW who has been a therapist in southeast Michigan since 1994. Although she has worked with individuals, couples, families, and groups on a wide variety of mental health and substance abuse problems, her special gift is working with clients who have attention deficit disorder (ADD). As Cindy worked through her values, vision for herself, and skills, and then researched her client base, she zoomed in on one of the toughest problems facing adults with ADD—simply organizing themselves. Further, her research showed that many of us entrepreneur types suffer from ADD, and that our disorganized offices and days are putting us at a severe disadvantage relative to our competition.

Her discovery led Cindy to develop a whole new business called "Fresh Start." The tag line? "Permanent solutions to organizing problems—with a specialty in home office organizing." It's a niche nobody else had discovered and one that suits Cindy perfectly. Best of all, helping people organize their offices naturally leads to psychotherapeutic counseling and long-term relationships. This is the kind of shift that can happen when you decide to take the time to think about several crucial areas: the context within which you are building your business, your customers and their needs, and your competitors' strengths—in other words when you embrace marketing as one of your core functions.

DEFINITIONS

There's always a marketing guru, and that guru always exhorts us to pay attention to marketing as though our entire future rests on it. For this lifetime anyway, he or she is right. Marketing is critical—maybe the most important function of your business once you figure out what the business is. If people don't know we're out there selling something, they can't buy whatever it is.

First, here's what marketing isn't: It isn't advertising. And it isn't sales. Although both are components of marketing, in a right livelihood business they come in at the tail end of your marketing tasks. Why? Because both are expensive. You want to be very certain about what you will do in advertising (if you do any at all) and how you will sell, before either get kicked into gear. The issue here is waste, and in a way, respect. To advertise or try to sell something to someone who doesn't need or want your products is disrespectful.

Here's a working definition of marketing: *it is your strategy for taking your product to market.* As such it is a "how," not a "what." It does, however, have specific components. They include:

1. Marketing objectives

2. An analysis of your market *and where it is headed.*

3. A plan for using the media.

4. A budget that both lists and prices all the resources that you will need to accomplish your marketing objectives.

Decades ago, when I was just starting out on this journey we call business building, I had the good fortune to take a marketing and sales class at IBM. It was the best class I have ever taken. The instructor, who reminded me of an army drill sergeant gone slightly astray, used to shout truisms at us. Given the sieve I call my brain, I've forgotten all of them but one: "*You people need to figure out what problem—exactly—you are solving with your product ....and how you are going to find the people (your customers) who have that problem.....and once you find them how you will convince them that you are the best solution so they will buy from you.*"

He was right. Our job is to understand the point of our product or service so we can analyze who really needs it. Only then can real marketing kick in, because that is when we'll know where to focus our marketing efforts, and what we need to do.

Company Objectives

The place to start? Your company's core objective. This is what defines your company, establishing a means of coordinating company actions, providing standards for measuring results, and communicating what it is you are striving to accomplish.

The company objective is like an umbrella protecting all aspects of your business in that it creates the framework within which you'll make all of your major decisions, including those related to marketing.

Good company objectives have five attributes:

1. They have a time frame.

2. They are measurable.

3. They create a picture in your brain. In other words, you can "see" what they mean.

4. They are broad. In the best case they are broad enough to include all aspects of the business. This is very different from a sales objective, or a technology objective, or a personnel objective. Each of these is only aimed at a part of the company.

5. They are achievable.

Here are two examples of company objectives that demonstrate what I have been trying to say:

"By 2002 Company Hearthappy will be a leader in the medical industry related to heart disease through its development and distribution of state-of-the-art surgical instruments for heart surgeries."

"ParentCare Inc. will be the largest franchiser for day care centers for the elderly in the Midwest states of Michigan, Ohio, and Indiana by the year 2005."

If you don't have a core company objective, now is the time to try one out on the worksheet provided. This is important because all of your marketing needs to be consistent with the objective, and to support it completely.

Marketing Objectives

Many people get carried away with these. In a right livelihood company, it is probably better to err on the side of having fewer, as in one to three, marketing objectives, rather than more than you can realistically support. I always start with one overriding marketing objective and if that doesn't get me to where I want to go, I add more, one at a time.

Here's how to come up with marketing objectives: Think about your market. Now ask yourself the following: What is the most important thing I need to do so my customers will know I am out here and will buy what I am selling? Is it:

1. Increase customer awareness?

2. Decrease resistance to buying from me?

3. Both 1 and 2?

Then write a statement that says how you will either increase awareness or decrease resistance. Yes, if you want to do both, two statements work just fine. I'll write the start of both types of objectives so you can fill in the blanks:

1. In (year), I will increase customer awareness by

_____

_____

_____

_____

2. In (year), I will decrease customer resistance to buying my products by

_____

_____

_____

_____

If I have done my job well, once you've gone through this chapter you will probably want to revisit what you just wrote.

I am always changing my marketing objectives based on additional information. I may shift from writing press releases for newsletters to signing up for a particular sales banner on the net. What matters is that your eye is always on the target market that you *know is yours*.

Then match their needs with your marketing campaigns and activities.

THE ENVIRONMENTAL ANALYSIS

The first step in developing a specific marketing strategy is to perform an environmental analysis. In other words, you want to consider the things that surround you—your context—so you can make an educated guess as to how it could impact your efforts. The "external environment" is important because it represents the "uncontrollables" in all of our lives.

Basically we live in four overlapping environments: the economic environment; our legal/political environment; the social/cultural environment; and the technological environment. As you research all four you'll discover problems and opportunities because *each environment affects the buying behavior of your customers.* Here's an example: Are you building an environmentally sensitive wood stove business? In a cold climate where wood is plentiful, people may buy more stoves than in a warmer climate. More people may buy the stoves where environmental laws are enforced. On the other hand, you might also have a lot more competition than if you position yourself as the only wood stove company in a mostly moderate climate.

At the same time, each of these environments is always changing. As a result, you need to periodically stop to check in on the patterns/trends in each. What trends, you ask? As many as you can stand to track. I've listed some of the major ones I try to study in the next section. Since there are many more, please try to add the pertinent ones to what you see in this workbook.

Economic Environment

Regarding the economic environment, what you are really after is a sense of the total business climate. Sources of data that are (mostly) user-friendly include:

Fortune, The Wall Street Journal, The Economist, the business section of your local newspaper, and regional business magazines. What matters is trends: What is increasing? Decreasing? Staying the same? And what do these patterns mean to your business? I guarantee they'll have some implications.

Larkin's favorite indicators:

1. Gross Domestic Product

2. Productivity Indices

3. Consumer Price Index

4. Unemployment Rates

5. Operating Profits

6. Purchasing Patterns

7. Inflation Rates

8. Consumer Spending Statistics.... at least the ones I understand.

Also check out your own industry. What is the current demand for products? What are their life cycles these days? In other words, how frequently are existing products or services replaced by "new, improved" versions? What emerging technology is moving into the industry? Are there changing customer profiles? For example, are new age groups suddenly interested in the products offered by the industry? New ethnic groups? What is the frequency of new product introductions? How about distribution patterns? Is everyone else on the Internet?...and anything else that matters to you (and that you have the energy to research).

Legal/Political Environment

The shape the country is in legally and politically impacts every business as well. It is important not to forget that the government continues to make rules, set limits, allocate and absorb resources...and as it does so, it creates opportunities for some of us and threats to others. An example: A single change in speed limits leads to different cars purchased, different tourism patterns, etc. You need to know what government agencies affect you and what regulations are about to make your life miserable (even if you agree with them in theory).

If you are exporting, you'll need to scope out the rules/customs of every country where you are exporting and save every penny you can to hire someone who has successfully exported to those countries to coach you through the roadblocks you'll face. Because they'll be there—providing you with an excellent opportunity to deepen your practice of patience.

Sociocultural or Demographic Environment

In the end, *people* have to say yes to us if we are going to succeed. That is why demographic trends are critical. Places to look for them include *American Demographics* magazine, John Naisbitt's *Trend Report*, *People* magazine (really!), and the writings of futurists such as Faith Popcorn and Watts Wacker.

Having said all this, there appear to be a number of megatrends out there that are going to impact how we all do business and to whom we sell our products:

- The aging population. More than thirty-four million of us will be over sixty-five years old by the year 2000. In fact, the fastest growing group is over 85 years old. Seventy-six million baby boomers are turning fifty right about now. On the other hand, there seems to be a shortage of 24- to 35-year-olds (which means that a whole lot of companies will need to outsource functions since they can't find employees).

- We are all single longer, and many of us are single more often. The median age for marriage is inching toward 30; more than a third of all adults live alone. Some demographers say that fewer than a fourth of all of our families have two parents and two kids. The moral of this story? Be sensitive to these trends when you consider putting pictures of people and families on your marketing materials.

- Women are working...more and more in our own businesses.

- As a society we are increasingly multicultural and multiethnic. The fastest growing group? Hispanic. The United States is now the fifth-largest Spanish-speaking country in the world. More than 28 million Hispanics live in the U.S. today, and they have an annual purchasing power of $230 billion. And this is a market with unique characteristics: it is young (median age 26), households are larger than is true for other ethnic groups, and households tend to be multigenerational and multi-familial. Here is just one impact of this trend: Spanish language programming is the fastest growing format in radio. The other ethnic group that is growing is made up of Asian households. Part of this is the result of increased Asian immigration to the United States.

- Concern about the natural environment and the condition it is in continues to grow, particularly among young adults.

- We are increasingly spiritually driven, although that doesn't necessarily mean that we've all gone back to church or, for those of us who have gone back to church, that they are the ones we grew up in.

- Anxiety is ever present. There is so much change in our lives, all the time, that our days feel increasingly chaotic—because they are. Planning becomes harder and harder. Less and less is predictable. The result? At best, low-grade anxiety in the calmest among us. At worst, high-level panic attacks.

- We want meaning in our lives. I think this is the result of all the baby boomers turning fifty. At any rate, it's a huge trend. Time is becoming more valuable than money. And the younger the worker, the more likely he or she will simply walk off the job if they want time to think or feel like what they are doing is meaningless.

- Faith Popcorn, one of the most user-friendly futurists around, says that trends such as cocooning (making nests of our houses), clanning (creating extended families and then spending all of our time with them), fantasy adventures, femalethink, cashing out (getting off the fast track), and down aging (clinging to our youth—I wish) are all trends that are here to stay. For better explanations of her trends, it's worth your time to read her recent book, *Clicking*.

Figuring Out Fads: The Five-Step Marathon

Trends are easy to spot because they take some time to surface and then grow to their height and stay there for awhile before they start to fade. As every entrepreneur knows, however, it is one thing to know the trends and incorporate them into what we do and another thing to actually *get the attention* of all those people or companies who have the problem we can solve. This is where fads come in. Getting potential customer attention means having something about you or what you are doing that is "hot" in their eyes. Why? Because the thirteen-year-old who still lives inside of each of us will be forever attracted to the popular crowd and companies that are hot are just that. Popular. They have a buzz about them that the rest of us want.

Happily, right livelihood businesses are already inherently hot because they reflect many of the trends that matter to all of us, notably protecting the environment and offering meaning to our lives. Even so, we need to offer other clues that reflect how "hot" we are so the interest of potential customers is piqued.

Unfortunately what is hot can shift pretty quickly—every six months or so in a consumer-driven economy. As a result, while we may not want to change our logo or marketing tag line every six months, we do need to think about other things we can do to "stay fresh." Maybe it is the color of our stationery. Maybe it is the format of our Website. Maybe it's a different-sized product line. How about "Bubble Baths for One" in recycled jars? Maybe it is a shift in where you advertise. Or how. Although these are not big changes, they can have a major impact on your marketing success.

Now comes the hard part. How does one figure out what is hot in the first place? Happily there is a research method that will work for anyone. At least that is my experience. And yes, let me admit this up front. It is not as refined as if you had thousands of analysts working for you á la Faith Popcorn... but it works better than people expect. The proof is in the trying.

Here are the five tasks: Every six months you'll need to set aside a day and a half of your time to undertake your own "Five Step Marathon." During this period, pretend that you have morphed into a walking, talking camcorder whose mission it is to uncover patterns of what people care about—and like—RIGHT NOW. (Yes, the patterns are pretty consistent across age groups. The older your market, however, the more muted the fad. Here's an example: If wide-legged jeans are hot for teens right now, they will also be hot for adults. But instead of the 40-inch-wide legs the teens want, full-blown adult jeans will only be a couple of inches wider than last year's pair.)

The actual five tasks?

1. Spend an afternoon at the most exclusive mall within driving distance. Gape at everything. If you are like me, you'll need to occasionally remind yourself to close your mouth. Every two hours, sit down and note the patterns you are seeing. For example: Which stores had the most shoppers in them? What were they buying? Are the stores crammed full of products or do they have a sense of spaciousness? Are things neat or messy? What colors are dominant? How about textures?

2. Spend an afternoon at the public library and/or on the Net and pretend you have to write an essay entitled, "The United States Today." Write down the key themes you discover by thumbing through economic and demographic reports or any findings of any major federal commissions—things like that. If you don't have time for this step, reading *U.S.A. Today* cover to cover for a couple of days works pretty well as an information source. You just need to remember to jot down dominant themes each time you read the paper so you can see the patterns that emerge.

3. Surf magazines. Lots of them—and not just the ones you normally read. Don't read, just look. What are the themes of the articles? What shows up in the ads? My all-time favorites: *Architectural Digest, Utne Reader, Jane, Wired, Fast Company, Emerge, Esquire,* European *Vogue* (French or Italian will do), and any of the major computer-related magazines. It is also a valuable exercise to skim through any magazines that your customer base reads. Again, write down the patterns that surfaced for you.

4. Watch this week's top ten prime-time TV shows and stay tuned to the commercials. Also check out any new shows that are getting a lot of press. What are the themes? What are the visuals? For example, are

pets everywhere? Are there lots of words in ads or just pictures? How about movement? Are particular types of people getting lots of TV time, such as single, young, intense urban professionals who are almost as neurotic as we are? Look for patterns.

5. Study the current *New York Times* bestsellers, reading a couple if you have time. These are important because they are read by opinion leaders, and opinion leaders have a lot to do with what ends up being "hot" in our culture. Cruise Oprah's current list of favorites as well. Then note the patterns—what are the themes that show up again and again? Whose voice is telling the stories? Are they first-person narrators or relatives of the main character? Are the stories funny, sad, traumatic, gross?

When you do the five steps and then sit down with your notes, you will be amazed at how obvious "hot" themes are. You'll even be able to tell what colors are the emerging hot colors. Scary, isn't it? Just as an example, here is a taste of the themes that have been "hot" at various times in the last decade:

Fall 1990: rap, scenery (think bucolic), marbleized everything, humor, green colors

Spring 1994: Day-Glo everything, streamlined, orange

Summer 1997: integrity, retro-fun (think Nick at Nite), safety

Fall 1998: extreme, edgy humor (usually pointed at self), ordinariness with a high-tech tinge and a touch of everyday heroism, romance

Technological Environment

Once you've reviewed people trends and examined fads and come up with ideas for how you could integrate those fads into what you are doing, it is worth your time to consider the present state of technology. Since ninety percent of all of the scientists who ever lived are alive today, tinkering away in a lab somewhere as you read this, technology will continue to evolve at high speed. Right now, new technology feels like it has about a two-year life cycle. And in that period, whatever technology you are thinking about will decrease in cost by about half, decrease in size by about the same amount, and double its capacity. It will typically become significantly more user-friendly at the same time.

There are a great many technological trends that will affect our businesses in some way. They are worth exploring as much as you can stand to, since, increasingly, our competition is technology instead of other people. Witness the accounting industry. It was hard hit by all the accounting software that keeps appearing, and the easier the software gets, the more trouble accountants are in.

Here are some of the significant trends related to technology:

- Miniaturization

- Mergings (computers/TV/Internet...gotta love those satellite dishes)

- Prices falling

- Everyone uses it (whether we want to or not).

- Easier to use (Happily, technology developers are figuring out that none of us read the manuals until we're in real trouble.)

- Internet rules: By 2004, everyone on the planet could have an Internet address if the pace of growth holds.

- Microsoft will continue to drive all standards from customer service, to corporate culture, to product life cycle expectations. (One woman's opinion. And yes, I do know about that guy in Finland.)

Emerging technologies? Laptops are becoming better and thinner. (We'll all be asking for the newest generation of Palm Pilots for Christmas if we aren't already. In fact, some of us will celebrate Christmas just to have this opportunity.) We also have the following to look forward to: really good voice recognition, networks of all shapes and sizes, voice-text-image improvements, video telephones (sorry), media explosions (120 channels is nothing.), smart houses/appliances/cars.

MARKET ATTRIBUTES

Customers

Market Segment Characteristics Enough about background information. Once you've made it through all of the research related to your business, you can start to define your market. Trying to do this before you look at trends and fads is incredibly dangerous. Why? Because, without some research, you and I only see what we want to see, and if I had more time I would go on and on about this but since I don't you'll just have to take my word for it or go out and read the chapter on mind games in *Stumbling Toward Enlightenment.*

Back to the task at hand. It is now possible to describe the *chunk* of population that you believe will buy your product. In other words, we aren't quite to the part where you describe the customers themselves—this is about *the group and the characteristics of the group.* I try to look at ten characteristics. Again, there are lots more if you want to keep going, but these ten have always worked pretty well for me.

1. What is the actual size of the group you want to sell to, in terms of money or units sold annually?

2. What is the rate of growth of this segment? How much more do they buy every year?

3. How long has this group been around? Have they just emerged or have they been buying products or services like yours for a long time?

4. If they buy one product or service, will they buy more?

5. How sensitive is this group to outside factors such as government regulations? If possible, you obviously want to find a segment that isn't sensitive. Otherwise, one change in regulation, or whatever the group is sensitive to, and you are out of business.

6. How sensitive is the group to price changes? This is a bit tricky. We were all raised to *say* that we are very sensitive to price, but the reality is that most of us aren't nearly as sensitive as we say we are and will gladly trade price sensitivity for things like convenience and con-

sistency any day. *Watch the behavior* of your market here…don't just take their word for it.

7. The seasonality of the group: When do they actually buy? This is important because you want to be marketing before then, so you'll be at your phone or computer to take orders during the buying season.

8. Is the group made up of cliques, and, if it is, are you a member? If you aren't, you may want to consider a different market segment.

9. How easy is it to sell to this segment? In a way, you don't want it to be *too* easy or everyone else who is potential competition will be able to sell to the group.

10. How much is technology a part of the lives of your customers? Your use of technology needs to match theirs if this is going to work.

There are many resources for this kind of information. My first step is always to surf the Web to see what I can dig up. Or you can approach industry associations for information. The U.S. Department of Commerce puts together excellent reports on market segments, as do financial analysts for major investment firms. If you get stuck, talk to your public library's information desk librarian. He or she will have ideas.

Specific Customers Within the boundaries of ethics, not to mention the law, you can't know your customers too intimately. Once you have a sense of the market segment you want to go after, you can think about the specific customers who make up that market. The starting place is to sit quietly and think about your perfect customer. Then, putting pen to paper or fingers to keyboard, list his or her characteristics. I actually start with the *person* who will say yes to me and then think about the company that will say yes to me if I am also selling to companies.

A perfect customer, as a reminder, is someone who knows they have the problem you can solve with your product, wants a solution, and will make a buying decision quickly. (I have had at least two friends who have almost gone bankrupt waiting for a "yes" from a huge corporate client's purchasing agent.) A sane rule of thumb is to get the initial clients first so you can feed yourself and your loved ones while you wait for the bigger buyers.

Back to listing the characteristics of your perfect customer. You want to do this, and here's why: once you have focused your energy on this group of people and companies or institutions, you can let go of picturing all of the other people in the world as potential customers and stop lying awake at night trying to figure how to get too many people's attention when your time could be better spent in quiet meditation or prayer. Concentrate on your first ten customers. Who will they be? Describe them in writing, without limiting yourself to the obvious indicators such as age, sex, and income. Instead include behavioral patterns, as well as lifestyle characteristics. Where do they live? Do they only have one home? How big is it? Where is it? What kind of a vehicle do they drive? Where do they go to church? Do they coach girls' basketball?

If you aren't simply selling to individuals, you repeat the same thinking to figure out which companies to focus on. I always consider attributes like: the age of the company; employment numbers and patterns, including whether they hire mostly young people; education levels of staff; profitability; type of business; their product lines; research and development expenditures; their geographical market; purchasing process; buying behavior (do they expect little gifts such as candles, chocolate, cigars?); and loyalty.

I can't say this too often: Your target customers know they have a problem, want a solution, have the money to pay for it, and will say yes quickly relative to other segments you could sell to. Don't spread yourself too thinly. A good segment (also called a market niche in the other business books you may be reading) will be pretty easily identifiable, will have potential, and will be accessible to you. The people who make up the market should also react uniquely to your marketing efforts. In other words, there is some way of telling from people's reactions to your marketing efforts whether they are a part of the segment or not.

Competition

Next to knowing what your customers want, the most important skill in marketing is figuring out what your competition is doing and what that means for you. *Everyone has competition.* About six years ago, I had a great idea for a service that I decided I could sell internationally and still live in a cave chanting away most of my days. It was a quarterly marketing newsletter on what was really "hot" to consumers. Did we all want spicier food, slower sex, sport-utility vehicles, ginseng gum? I figured I would make it a fun read with lots of pictures and "proofs" of the trends in the form of pictographs and mini-stories. Plus, as an extra added bonus, I would enclose a small gift—something that personified what was "hot" at the time. For example, if I were sending out the newsletter in the fall of 1998, I'd probably enclose Web Fuels—small metal tins of near-pain-inducing mints that also happen to have a list of really great Internet sites printed on the inside of the tin. Web Fuels merge taste—extreme taste—with the Web. At the same time, they are the perfect "small indulgence," another "hot" trend. For $2.95 I could give my clients' taste buds a run for their money, clear out the java taste for awhile, *and* save time hunting down new places to play on the Internet. It doesn't get better cheaper.

Anyway, I did a mock-up of the newsletter and sent it out to potential customers. They loved it and, happily, suggested a price range of $195 to $280 for an annual subscription. With a printer identified and mailing costs stashed, I casually started to analyze my competition, confident that I was unique in the universe. And realized, with a week, that the newsletter wouldn't make it. First I noticed that *American Demographics* was covering more and more of what I planned to write about. Then new magazines started to pop up all around me with the same stuff—*Wired*, then *Fast Company*—and they were just the start. Then I got onto the Web and discovered that not only was my data available, it could be accessed in seconds (on a good day), 24 hours a day. And it was up-to-the-minute. I didn't even bother to look at what marketing information industry associations provide for their members. Instead I got a job while I regrouped. Looking back, as frustrated as I was, without the competitive analysis I would have thrown as much as $20,000 at a sure failure.

We all have competition. Right now, yours is how your customers are currently solving the problem you want to solve with your products or services. And, for better or worse, their existing solution is a habit...one you need to help them break if they are going to turn to you instead.

It is worth every minute you spend figuring out exactly who your competition is. It is also important to track what they do. *How to Drive Your Competition Crazy* by Guy Kawasaki offers some useful ideas about this. Ask your existing or potential customers who your competitors are and what they like and don't like about them. If your competitors are other companies, go to trade shows to scope them out. Get industry newsletters. Read about them. Order something from them so you can see their written materials, then test out their customer service and see how efficient they are.

Here are some of the things you will want to compare: price, performance, warranties, reputation, market share, and why your customers buy from them. If your competition isn't other people, you still need to do the analysis. I once worked with a technology-based company that made security systems. Their toughest competition (and it took us awhile to figure this one out) was guard dogs. When we did the competitive analysis it was clear that they wouldn't be able to neutralize the benefits of the dogs so they sold their technology and moved on.

Positioning

Everything we have done so far is really geared toward one goal—to figure out what your position (or sustainable identification) is in your market. Customers choose products based on the *benefits* they expect the product to deliver. It is that simple. For example, a product such as a computer training program may be expected to be efficient (not waste time), entertaining, and timely. An herbal remedy might be judged by its freshness, the speed at which it works, ease of use, lack of side effects, and access to a help line.

What matters to your customers? What will they use to compare you with your competition? Here are some examples of the benefits of a product or service that your customers might mention if they were in the room with you right now: fair price, service before and after a sale, user-friendly technology, quality, product applications (all the different ways the product can be used), distribution channels (how the product will get to them), consistency, time savings (efficiency), convenience, privacy...you get the idea.

Given the benefits that matter to your customers, where do you stand relative to your competition? When you figure that out (try not to guess), you know your market position. And once you know your position, you need to make certain that everything you do is consistent with it. So if you are the one with the highest quality, then your people, product, services, printed materials, office spaces, address, automobiles, and everything else you can think of that is related to your business need to be elegant. If you are the competitor perceived to provide "the best service" you may need to answer your phone around the clock and return phone calls within the hour if not sooner. You can also expect to give your clients your home phone number.

NITTY GRITTY DETAILS

Once you've figured out your market position, the rest of marketing is straightforward. In a perfect world, this would be where you actually design your product or services based on customer needs. Since none of us do that, you'll want to see what you can shift to better match what your customers are looking for...and then, step by step, starting where you are right now, make those changes.

Features and Benefits

First step? Take a look at the features of what you are selling—all of them—so you can move toward matching what your customers want if you aren't already there. There are two types of features to consider. Tangible features are the physical features related to what you sell that your customers can measure with their senses. Do your words need to be bigger than normal so your older clients can see them? What about colors? Size? The paper you use for your marketing materials? The car you drive? (Yes, I know I keep bringing up cars. I didn't realize I am still so easily obsessed.) Pay attention to consistency.

If you are building a right livelihood business, another helpful exercise is to think about whether the tangible features match your own values. Smell matters more and more these days. We all want whatever we buy to have a clean smell. The sound of your product or service also comes in here. (Yes, that does bring me to voice mail and e-mail. If our growing irritation at voice mail barriers and e-mail busyness continues, the companies that have a real person answering the phone or taking messages may end up being the real success stories in their markets as we cross the threshold to the next millennium.)

Other features are intangible. These are subjective and have to do with the less visible benefits we offer our customers or clients. Are the dishes cleaner? Is the water safe? Right now the most frequent concern I hear is whether or not the customer believes he or she has made a safe decision when they say yes to us. It is that anxiety trend, poking its nose into the buying decision.

If you are unclear about any of this — what your customers want, or who your competitors are and why, try doing a focus group with potential clients to see what they have to say. You can do it yourself if you have to. Just check out some basic marketing books from the library for guidelines.

Price

The big issue here is making sure that you charge enough for your product or service to make a profit. Here's one way to figure out price:

1. What does it cost you to produce each unit of product or service you are selling? (Don't forget to put a dollar value on your time. For example, if your time is worth $35 an hour to you and it takes three hours to develop a training module for a client, then the cheapest price you could ever offer is 3 times $35, or $105 per module.)

2. What are the overhead expenses that need to be included in the price of each product? (Rent, utilities, phone costs, etc.)

3. The sum of one and two is the minimum you can charge and still live.

4. For sanity's sake, add some profit for yourself into the price (mostly because there will be costs neither of us has thought of). Then, staring at the number you've come up with, ask yourself: Is my market really price sensitive? (Probably not as much as you used to think before you got to know them.) Could I sell for less than my competition and still make a profit? The answer is usually no.

5. You'll need to add in marketing costs per unit as well. Marketing isn't free.

This last sum is your price per unit. Please don't discount unless you are starving to death, because once you discount your product, that becomes your de facto price.

Once you start selling your product, here are some warning signs that the price you've come up with is too low:

- Profits are getting smaller on the same or rising number of sales.

- Prices are significantly lower than competition in spite of all my nagging.

- Customers are always telling you how good or how much better run your company is than your competitors.

- Nobody complains about your prices (or a customer takes you aside to tell you your prices are too low).

- You haven't changed your prices for ages.

- People buy without asking about price or haggling.

- Customers buy more than they need and you know it.

Distribution

Distribution is about how you actually get your product into the hands of your clients. Do you sell directly to them or use a middleman? Right livelihood businesses work hard to sell directly to their clients whenever and however they can. Here's why: Middlemen can cause you to miss critical opportunities to collect crucial market information, such as what else you could sell to solve their problems. This is not information that is purposefully overlooked by the middlemen. It's just that nobody cares about this as much as you do, so they won't pick up on as many clues.

If you need to be convinced of these particular blunt opinions, read *The One to One Future* by Don Peppers and Martha Rogers. You can't get too close to your customers and that is all there is to that.

Packaging

Be careful about the image you project to your customers and remember this: *A negative image in your market is impossible to fix.* Packaging starts with the name of your firm, includes the names of your products or services, and moves out to embrace every decision you make related to image: logo, packaging, the words you use, lettering. Don't guess. Check all of your decisions out with potential clients before anything is finalized. It will save you lots of time, money, and energy later.

Public Relations

My experience is that people who do well with public relations don't need to do much advertising—maybe none. In a nutshell, public relations is the fine art of getting three audiences to know and love you: the media where your market segment gets its information, your community because that is where your reputation is made, and your customers.

What is wonderful about public relations is that the media becomes the channel of communication between you and potential clients at low or no cost to you. (I love this.) What to do? Step number one is to become an expert in your industry. How? By feeding useful information to the reporters who are writing or reporting in the media that your clients use. That way reporters will quote you as an expert in your field (which you are). If your clients are readers, you feed the information to newspapers, journals, selective Net sites, and magazines. If they are radio listeners, you feed it to radio personalities until they invite you to be a guest. If they watch the news...you know the drill.

If being an expert doesn't get you all the clients or customers you want, you'll need to learn to write a press release. Basically, a press release is a one-page summary that announces news about you. Maybe you opened a division. Maybe you have a new client. Maybe you replanted the entire rain forest. What you want to do is summarize your excitement about this momentous occasion in a format that says:

1. What you are excited about (In other words, what is the big deal here?);

2. Why you are excited;

3. Who it is exactly that is so excited; ·

4. Where all this excitement is going on;

5. When all this hit; and

6. How someone can get more information.

It's that simple. Again, there are numerous books out there that can help you with this. Head for the library again, or ask around. Someone you know has written a press release.

Every time you hit a milestone (opening for business counts as a big one), do a press release about it and send it to the pertinent reporters you have already identified, along with an interesting photo. If the media doesn't bite immediately, don't worry. Just keep at it. If, however, you try five or six press releases with no luck, call a key reporter or editor for advice on what you could do better. For most of us the combination of expertise (which lends itself to your being quoted quite frequently) and press releases lead to decent exposure in your market. The result? Exactly the customers you were hoping for! And plenty of them.

On the chance that you don't get all the exposure and customers you want by this point, try a direct mail campaign where you write a *personal letter* to each potential client that summarizes how you can solve the problem you have identified. (Yes, I really mean personal. If you find yourself mentally whining about this, go back to chapter one and reread the precepts, then come back to this section.) Follow up with a phone call and even if you get voice mail leave a message or two, then leave the potential customer alone. After that a letter or note or media article every six months or so is a gentle reminder that you are out there happily solving other clients' problems. Unless a competitor is really doing a better job, it is only a matter of time before you are working for that client.

If you are impatient and don't want to wait for the process I have just described to unfold, you can advertise as well. Before you decide, let me just say that all of our lives are so busy that it will typically take us quite a few times (as in eight to ten...or even more) before we even notice an advertisement aimed directly at us. Please budget accordingly and think about this decision a couple of times. How can you best save resources and still get customer attention? It could take a totally unique form of advertising. (Such as beautiful chimes made out of recycled materials that have your marketing message on them and are hung in public places. The possibilities are endless.)

To finish up here, the best way I know to tie all of the various aspects of marketing together is to make yourself a one-page summary of all your key marketing decisions, and a timeline of what needs to be done when. Then you are on your merry way. Good luck and Buddhaspeed.

A DEFINITION OF MARKETING

Remember that 80 percent of marketing is research!

_____

_____

_____

_____

_____

_____

_____

_____

_____

_____

Your marketing mantra: Who has the problem I am solving with my product?

_____

_____

_____

_____

_____

_____

_____

_____

_____

_____

_____

_____

COMPANY OBJECTIVES

Try Yours Here:

_____

_____

_____

_____

_____

_____

Marketing objectives for the next year

1. I will increase the awareness of my market of my products (services) by:

    _____

    _____

    _____

    _____

    _____

    _____

    _____

2. I will decrease resistance to purchasing my products (services) by:

    _____

    _____

    _____

    _____

    _____

    _____

THE ENVIRONMENTAL ANALYSIS

1. What are the economic trends right now? (Consider national, regional and local trends.)

_____

_____

_____

_____

_____

_____

_____

_____

_____

_____

How will these trends affect your business?

_____

_____

_____

_____

_____

_____

_____

_____

_____

_____

_____

2. What about legal and political trends?

_____

_____

_____

_____

_____

_____

_____

_____

_____

_____

Which trends will have an impact on you?
What do you think the impact will be?

_____

_____

_____

_____

_____

_____

_____

_____

_____

_____

3. What about sociocultural, or people, trends? What are they?

_____

_____

_____

_____

_____

_____

_____

_____

_____

_____

_____

What impact will they have on you?

_____

_____

_____

_____

_____

_____

_____

_____

_____

_____

_____

_____

4. What about technology? What are the trends?

_____

_____

_____

_____

_____

_____

_____

_____

_____

_____

_____

What do they mean for you? What shifts in technology do you need to make to keep up with your market?

_____

_____

_____

_____

_____

_____

_____

_____

_____

_____

FIGURING OUT FADS:
THE FIVE-STEP MARATHON

1. Mall observations:

_____

_____

_____

_____

_____

2. What matters right now:

_____

_____

_____

_____

_____

3. Magazine themes:

_____

_____

_____

_____

_____

4. TV and commercial themes:

_____

_____

_____

_____

5. The books:

_____

_____

_____

_____

_____

_____

_____

_____

What's hot now?

1. _____

2. _____

3. _____

4. _____

5. _____

What little changes can you make in marketing or how you do business so you're "hot" too?

_____

_____

_____

_____

_____

_____

_____

_____

MARKET ATTRIBUTES

(Remember, what we're talking about here is the chunk of population you are after, not the individual characteristics of your customers.)

1. _____

_____

_____

_____

2. _____

_____

_____

_____

3. _____

_____

_____

_____

4. _____

_____

_____

_____

5. _____

_____

_____

_____

6. _____

_____

_____

_____

7. _____

_____

_____

_____

8. _____

_____

_____

_____

9. _____

_____

_____

_____

10. _____

_____

_____

_____

THE PERFECT CUSTOMER

Now we're after the characteristics of your perfect customer. Here are some clues to help you think about him/her. (Why yes, this exercise could help you to figure out who an appropriate mate would be as well. Just so you know.)

Activities: work, hobbies, social events attended, vacation, entertainment, clubs, community, shopping, sports

Interests: family, home, job, community, recreation, fashion, food, media, achievements

Opinions: themselves, social issues, politics, business, economics, education, products, future, culture

Demographics: age, education, income, occupation, family size, dwelling, geography, city size

All right, start listing their characteristics. Try to make yourself list as many as twenty. Often it is the less obvious characteristics that help you to isolate unique ways to find and then get the attention of your customers. For example, if your perfect customers are married, live in wealthier neighborhoods, and have adolescents, you might want to do some entertaining school program for the kids that they tell their parents about...or you can send them home with samples.

Characteristics

1. _____

2. _____

3. _____

4. _____

5. _____

6. _____

7. _____

8. _____

9. _____

10. _____

11. _____

12. _____

13. _____

14. _____

15. _____

16. _____

17. _____

18. _____

19. _____

20. _____

Try to keep going if you can. Also, if you are selling to companies or organizations, you should repeat the exercise, only this time you will describe the company instead of the person who will say yes. In this case you want to think about things like the size of the company, number of employees, etc.

WHAT BENEFITS MATTER THE MOST TO MY CUSTOMERS?

1. Price

2. Quality

3. Consistency

4. Service

5. Wide variety of choices

6. Psychological reward of ownership

7. Personalization

8. Other _____

Remember that they'll probably say price matters the most. What they actually do will tell you more about what is critical to them.

THE COMPETITION

	Strengths	Weaknesses	Neutralizing the Strengths
1. Name			
Address			
Contact			
Phone			
Other pertinent information:			
2. Name			
Address			
Contact			
Phone			
Other pertinent information:			
3. Name			
Address			
Contact			
Phone			
Other pertinent information:			

	Strengths	Weaknesses	Neutralizing the Strengths
4. Name			
Address			
Contact			
Phone			
Other pertinent information:			
5. Name			
Address			
Contact			
Phone			
Other pertinent information:			
6. Name			
Address			
Contact			
Phone			
Other pertinent information:			

MARKET POSITION

Where do you fit relative to your competition?

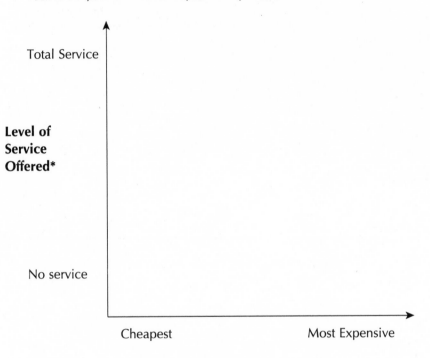

Product Price*

*Remember that these dimensions need to be the two benefits that really matter the most to your customers. Please don't guess at this.

NITTY GRITTY DETAILS

1. Tangible features

   _____

   _____

   _____

   _____

   _____

   _____

2. Intangible features

   _____

   _____

   _____

   _____

   _____

   _____

3. Pricing that makes sense given your marketing research: What price makes the most sense to you?

   _____

   _____

   _____

   Why?

   _____

   _____

   _____

4. Distribution

_____
_____
_____
_____
_____
_____
_____
_____
_____
_____

5. Packaging. Some say image is everything.

_____
_____
_____
_____
_____
_____
_____
_____
_____
_____

PUBLIC RELATIONS

What will you do to get the attention of:

1. The media?

_____
_____
_____
_____
_____
_____

2. The community?

_____
_____
_____
_____
_____
_____

3. Customers?

_____
_____
_____
_____
_____
_____

Please be as specific as you can stand to be. Include deadlines for yourself or this stuff won't get done.

Chapter Six

Financial Considerations

(If you have no familiarity with finance terms, you might want to first review the "Glossary of Financial Terms" sheet at the tail end of this chapter. It should take some of the scariness out of thinking about finances. At least it does for me when I look at it.)

CASH FLOW

I'm not going to tell you all the horror stories that unfold when business owners don't pay attention to the financial side of their business, because I continue to hope that they can rise out of their own ashes. I have stood beside clients while they watched their store doors padlocked and I have watched relationships crumble when a business run by one of the partners drives them into bankruptcy. Families have exploded over unwise money moves, and I even spent the better part of a year visiting one of my favorite clients in jail.

Here's the bottom line with money and a right livelihood business: Your cash flow is everything. Before you shrug that this is just one more rant from me, here are some words from a well regarded consultant and frequent contributor to *Inc.* magazine, Norm Brodsky:

"There's a hard lesson we all have to learn when we go into business. The lesson is that you live or die on cash flow. Sales

117

are nice. Profits are even nicer. But it's cash flow that deter-mines whether or not you survive. Where most first time entre-preneurs trip up is in failing to understand that more sales almost always mean less cash flow—and less cash flow means trouble.

Believe me I speak from experience here. I had no concept of the relationship between sales and cash flow when I started my first company. I thought sales were everything. If someone came and offered me a million dollars' worth of new business my only question was 'When does it start?' I took all the business I could get as fast as I could get it and the company grew like crazy....We had cash flow problems all the way, but I didn't focus on them. I was too busy selling.

The whack on the head finally came in the form of a cash flow crunch that forced me to go without a salary for four straight weeks....What I learned was that you have to look ahead. You have to figure out how you're going to get the cash required to increase your sales at whatever rate you have in mind.... I'm talking about losing control of your situation, about decisions being taken away from you, about being forced to do extreme and unwise things just to stay alive." ("Paying for Growth", Norm Brodsky, Inc., October, 1996, p. 29)

The sample cash budget worksheet at the back of this chapter will help you to start framing the financial dimensions of your company. Doing the analysis on the sheet helps entrepreneurs to look ahead by esti-mating monthly income and expenses. At a minimum, you want to pro-ject out for a full year. The cash flow will tell you where the probable dry months will be, and whether you will need to borrow money to get started or expand.

To fill in the blanks, you'll have to make estimates. I would try to talk to owners of similar or comparable businesses to see if they can help you. A good banker usually has some cash flow models. Your accountant may have some ideas from her work with similar companies. Or you can see if your industry association has some model budgets. The worksheet, "How Much Money Do You Need?" will also help you think through budget issues. I've listed typical categories of ongoing costs as well as one-time start-up costs you may face. While every business is unique, you'll at least have a place to start using the line items I put on this sheet.

Happily, if you don't want to do this exercise by hand, there are a lot of software programs out there that can speed up the time needed to develop your cash flow. Most of the entrepreneurs I know are using some version of Quickbooks. Ask around.

The Records You Need to Keep

There are a number of records that need tracking when you are building a business. They help you to be efficient because you'll have a better sense of when money is coming in, and how, and when money is going out, and how. As such, they are also input for your cash flow estimates for next year.

A) Daily:

Buy ledgers or set up ledgers on your computer so you can account for:

1. Total cash on hand.

2. All your income for that day.

3. Any payments you made.

4. Any new inventory.

You'll also want to enter any deposits you make at your bank into your business checkbook, as opposed to your personal one. It is important to keep these separate. You should always have a sense of what your balance is.

B) Weekly:

1. Check your accounts receivable (people who owe you money) to see if you need to contact any slow payers. Ninety percent of the time a phone call will do. After that, write to them. After that, you'll need to decide. Anyone who takes longer than thirty days to pay you should make you nervous, unless longer payment times are an industry standard or you were warned in advance.

2. Review your accounts payable (money you owe) to see if there is anybody you owe money to who is expecting a payment right about now. I cannot tell you how critical it is to pay on time or slightly early if you can. Again, this is about respect and using resources efficiently. You don't want to force people to call or send reminders. If you don't or won't have the money you need to pay someone, call them early so you can work with them to figure out a payment plan. Most business owners have faced tough times themselves and will understand this, as long as they are forewarned so they can make their own plans.

3. Prepare payroll, if you have staff. *(I do not recommend hiring staff until you are absolutely certain that you need them. I would subcontract tasks just as long as I legally could.)* This can be a bit complicated. Most state governments offer free "how to prepare payroll" packages that they will send to you if you ask.

4. If you are making things, deduct any inventory you have sold from your inventory ledger.

Monthly:

1. Balance your checkbook. I try to stay within $5.00 of what the bank tells me I have.

2. Total all the ledgers that were listed in the daily tasks.

3. Start, and then add to, your stash of tax deposits so you aren't stunned by how much you'll have to come up with later.

4. If you are manufacturing products, review your inventory to see if you need to order anything, or organize a "fire sale" to get rid of some of your stock.

5. Reconcile your petty cash. In other words, make sure the actual cash, plus the total of the paid out receipts for expenses from petty cash, are equal to your starting balance. If you are like the rest of us, this will take a couple of months to get this one down. I'm always grabbing a couple of dollars from petty cash and then forgetting to get receipts. As a result, every once in a while I end up staring at a petty cash tin that is missing $100 to $200 with no idea where it all went. So get receipts. Otherwise you can find yourself lying awake at night wondering what happened. Also, you may discover you are using petty cash for things like office supplies, which are better paid for out of your business checking account.

Quarterly:

1. File your estimated federal and state tax returns (the ones your accountant helped you with). Depending on where you live, you may also have local taxes to pay.

2. Send any sales taxes you owe to your state and local governments (if the local government collects them—it depends on where you live).

3. Analyze your cash flow for the last quarter. Where were the surprises? What are their implications?

Annually:

1. Total all your ledgers and add up your yearly totals for all your various expenses and income categories.

2. Prepare an annual income statement so you can see how you are doing. This is simply a total of the last twelve months' actuals—what you actually made, instead of what you thought would happen.

3. Prepare your budget for the next twelve months.

4. Send out 1099 forms to all of your subcontractors and W-2 forms to staff. You can get these from your state government.

5. Pull together everything you need to pay your taxes and make an appointment with your accountant to plan anything you need to plan related to money.

6. Pay all your taxes so you don't go to jail.

THE BALANCE SHEET

Sometimes banks and other investors ask for a balance sheet. I don't do them unless someone makes me because I have more productive ways to use my time. Having whined, here's how you do one if it becomes a mandate. (It helps to look at the model balance sheet worksheet first, the one titled "Jamie's Organic Juice Stand.")

Basically, a balance sheet is simply a statement that reports the financial condition of your business on a particular date. Most people like to use the last day of their fiscal year which, for most of us, is December 31. Balance sheets always have the same format: assets on the left, liabilities and net worth or equity on the right. And the total assets always need to equal the sum of total liabilities and net worth. It took me a full year of accounting classes to realize that this is a truism of balance sheets. If you do this exercise and the two don't add, just increase the amount of the net worth until they do. In accountantese this increase is called a "plug."

Back to the sheet. Looking at the assets column, assets are *always* listed from the most liquid (in other words, dollars you can immediately get your hands on) at the top, to the least liquid (such as land, which you have to sell to get cash) at the bottom. Entries are also always grouped in two categories, current assets and fixed assets. Current assets represent cash and include things like bank account balances, accounts receivable, inventory, and any expenses you have prepaid. Fixed assets, on the other hand, tend to be things like equipment and buildings and land that you aren't going to try to convert into cash during the normal operation of your business. (If I have lost you right about now, go back and study the worksheet for a couple of minutes and then reread this section.)

The liabilities column on the right is also arranged in order of decreasing immediacy, from your most pressing bills (accounts payable) to the least pressing (any long-term loans you might have). These entries also have two categories: current liabilities are the bills you need to pay within the next twelve months while long term liabilities are typically multi-year loans.

The balance sheet tells us a lot. The assets you have to work with. How much debt you have hanging over your head. How much equity you have in the business. Why does equity matter? Because equity is one of the measures of added value, or success. Plus, the higher your company's net worth, the more you should be able to get when you decide to sell it.

SOURCES OF MONEY

What if you plot out an annual budget and draft up a balance sheet and it becomes excruciatingly clear that you will need to borrow money? Here are some time-proven sources of funding:

- If you are lucky enough to own a house, second mortgages are wonderful.

- You may be able to borrow from a retirement package you have in place.

- Your bank or credit union. These days the federal government is really trying to help us start enterprises and therefore have a number of useful programs toward that end. Good bankers know about them.

- Credit cards—for the truly brave.

- Lines of credit with your suppliers (so you don't have to come up with money up front).

- Gifts of money from relatives. (Try not to make it a loan for both your sakes. Relatives tend to be unskilled lenders. And you don't want to live with the repercussions of not paying back a loan in case your business doesn't do well. Which brings me to an important corollary: *Never, ever borrow money from someone who can't afford to lose it.*)

- Loans from other entrepreneurs who are very successful. This one is another favorite. Other business owners know what you are going through because they have been there. Just make sure he or she has an excellent reputation, and you trust him/her.

- Sell stuff. I've seen people start businesses with money raised from selling their art collection, jewelry, cars, and baseball cards. Sometimes a good garage sale can kick you into gear.

- Keep an eye out for other off-the-beaten-path loan funds. Like what? Like rural loan funds or like the community development block grant loan funds sitting in city and county buildings all over America. Like community development corporation loan funds. Finding them takes a little investigative work, but you're up to it if you've made it this far in the workbook. Start by calling city or county employees involved in economic development. *Guerrilla Financing* by Jay C. Levinson and Bruce Blechman (Houghton Mifflin) may trigger additional ideas.

THE LOAN PROPOSAL

If you decide that you want a loan from someone somewhere, it is worth the time it takes to put together a one-page loan proposal to frame your discussions. "The Loan Proposal" worksheet lists the components of a good proposal. You need to put a date on the proposal to get the ball rolling, and to be really clear about who is getting the money. Is it you? You and a partner? A business? The next big decision is the type of loan you want. Is it a term loan (in other words, one with a clear beginning and end), or are you going to try for a line of credit for which you'll pay interest only on the actual money you use?

What is the amount of the loan? (Add ten to twenty percent to what you think you need, because there is always something nobody thought of.) What will it be used for (use of proceeds) exactly? Let me say here that nobody will want to pay you back for any money you may have lent to the business yourself, so I wouldn't even try to go after this.

What is the term of the loan? Do you want a one-year loan, a three-year loan, a five-year loan? Try to stretch out the term for as long as you can so your monthly payments will be as low as possible in your early years.

Of the total amount you are requesting, how much do you want on the day of closing, i.e., when the lender writes you the check? Most of us don't need all the money right away.

The less you take up front, the lower your payments will be. It is just fine to ask for a specific and personalized paydown schedule. You might need to purchase inventory or buy equipment on a certain schedule. Get the money paid to you in a way that matches those dates.

Collateral is what you'll use to pay back the loan if the company doesn't make money as quickly as you think it will. It could be equipment you already own, another mortgage on your house, a family member who is willing to sign on as a back-up.

Rate of interest? As low as you can get away with. Period. As for the repayment schedule, again you can be as creative as you can negotiate. I always try to get a grace period (of, say, six months) before I have to start paying back a loan, and even then I may try to make interest-only payments for awhile until the business really kicks in and I can make bigger payments.

Most lenders ask for guarantees. This cracks me up since there are no guarantees in life, but the language of lending is the language of lending so you'll be expected to say something. Try starting out with "There is no need for any guarantees, as you can see from my business plan" and see how far you can get. In the end most of us end up giving personal guarantees which means that the lender will come after our personal assets if we don't repay the loan. Do what you have to do.

Outline the source of funds for repayment: that is, how your sales will cover all your costs. Your cash flow projections should help you to make your case here. If you want to be truly impressive you can come up with an extra credit back-up plan as well—such as promising to take a weekend job to pay back the loan if sales are slow, or naming another entrepreneur who could buy you out if you really needed cash quickly.

The closing date is when you want to get your initial check from the lender so you can start putting his/her money to use. Finally, as with the business plan, it is important to remember to put your name, address, and phone number on your proposal so the lender can call you with the invariable questions he/she will have.

Yes, getting loans is a lot of work—and it's time consuming. But if it is your only path to prosperity, then it is time to take the risk. If you mess up you probably have at least ten thousand lifetimes to make things right.

THE VALUE OF A CERTIFIED PUBLIC ACCOUNTANT

I know, I know, I am really harping on this point. It is because I don't want any right livelihood entrepreneurs to go to jail because they didn't follow regulations and laws. In the business world, ignorance of the law does not keep you out of jail. A good CPA can keep you safe relative to tax issues, making sure that you file reports and pay taxes when they are all due. He can also offer you consulting assistance relative to setting up, and then running, your business and can provide guidelines and insights related to your own personal finances. Please find one.

As a rule of thumb, it is a good idea to interview several potential accountants before you hire anyone. This person is someone that you will have to tell all of your secrets to—and with whom you will share all of your fears related to money. I have watched good accountants keep people in business and I have seen unskillful accountants cause havoc.

Questions for the interviews?

1. Have you worked with start-up (or small) businesses before? (You want a yes.)

2. What do you know about my industry? (Hopefully lots.)

3. What are your fees?

4. When do you bill?

5. Is there a reference I could talk to?

6. (Extra credit question) Who will actually be doing my work? (You can't afford a beginner.)

Have fun with this. I'll look for you in *Fast Company*.

ONE-YEAR CASH FLOW PROJECTIONS

Month	1	2
Income:		
Cash on hand (leftovers from last month)		
Payments from customers		
Other income		
Total:		
Payments:		
Purchases (such as supplies)		
Equipment purchases		
Wage expenses		
Subcontractor expenses		
Accounting/legal expenses		
Rent		
Utilities		
Phone		
Insurance		
Taxes		
Interest		
Repairs/maintenance		
Automotive		
Travel		
Loan repayments		
Other expenses		
Total:		
Income – payments = Cash balance at end of the month:		

3	4	5	6

Month	7	8
Income:		
Cash on hand (leftovers from last month)		
Payments from customers		
Other income		
Total:		
Payments:		
Purchases (such as supplies)		
Equipment purchases		
Wage expenses		
Subcontractor expenses		
Accounting/legal expenses		
Rent		
Utilities		
Phone		
Insurance		
Taxes		
Interest		
Repairs/maintenance		
Automotive		
Travel		
Loan repayments		
Other expenses		
Total:		
Income – payments = Cash balance at end of the month:		

9	10	11	12

THE BOOKS YOU NEED TO KEEP

1. Daily: _____
   _____
   _____
   _____

2. Weekly: _____
   _____
   _____
   _____

3. Monthly: _____
   _____
   _____
   _____
   _____

4. Quarterly: _____
   _____
   _____

5. Annually: _____
   _____
   _____
   _____
   _____
   _____

THE BALANCE SHEET

JAMIE'S ORGANIC JUICE STAND
BALANCE SHEET 12/31/99

ASSETS		LIABILITIES AND NET WORTH	
CURRENT ASSETS		**CURRENT LIABILITIES**	
Cash on hand	200	Accounts payable	200
Inventory		Bill for carrots	50
Carrots/juice		Rent of space	150
supplies	200	Short term debt	600
		12 x $50 for loan	
TOTAL:	$400	TOTAL:	$800
FIXED ASSETS		**LONG-TERM LIABILITIES**	
Equipment		Loan for garden plot	$100
Juice stand	100		
Juice equip.	100		
Garden			
Carrots	100		
Orange trees	500		
TOTAL			
FIXED ASSETS:	$800	TOTAL LIABILITIES:	$900
		NET WORTH:	$300
TOTAL		TOTAL LIABILITIES AND	
ASSETS:	$1,200	NET WORTH:	$1,200

HOW MUCH MONEY DO YOU NEED TO GET STARTED?

Item	Estimated annual cost
1. Your salary (You need a salary. This is no time to be a martyr.)	
2. All other costs related to people (salaries, taxes, subcontractors)	
3. Rent	
4. Advertising/marketing costs	
5. Delivery expenses	
6. Supplies	
7. Telephone	
8. Utilities	
9. Insurance	
10. Taxes related to the business	
11. Interest	
12. Maintenance	
13. Legal/accounting fees	
14. Dues/subscriptions	
15. Furniture/equipment costs	
16. Inventory purchases (if you are making things)	
17. Other costs (I haven't thought of)	
	Total:

ONE-TIME START-UP COSTS

Estimated cost

---

1. Equipment (phones, computers, faxes, vacuum cleaner, etc.)

2. Furniture

3. Decorating/remodeling

4. Starting inventory if you are making things

5. Office supplies

6. Rent and utility deposits

7. Licenses/permits

8. Advertising related to your grand opening or introduction of a new product line

9. Cash for emergencies

10. Other things I haven't thought of

Total:

SOURCES OF MONEY

You can use this page to list ideas you think of as you read this chapter, as well as ideas from anyone else who might know about raising money from their own experience. It is really helpful to keep a running list of ideas and to read books that might offer suggestions (or surf the Net).

LOAN PROPOSAL

1. The date you give the lender the proposal: _____

2. Person(s) borrowing the money: _____

3. Type of loan you want: _____

4. The amount of the loan (try to be specific): _____

5. How the loan will be used: _____

6. The length (term) of the loan: _____

7. How much you need at closing (this is the "takedown"): _____

8. Collateral: _____

9. Proposed interest rate: _____

10. Repayment schedule: _____

11. Any guarantees you can offer: _____

12. Source of funds for repayment
    (what your cash flow indicates): _____

13. An alternative source of funds for repayment: _____

14. The date you want to close the deal: _____

15. Information about the contact person
    (name, address, phone, fax, etc.): _____
    _____
    _____
    _____

THE VALUE OF A CERTIFIED
PUBLIC ACCOUNTANT (CPA)

1. Tax issues: _____

   _____

   _____

   _____

2. Management consulting: _____

   _____

   _____

   _____

3. Advice: _____

   _____

   _____

   _____

   Questions to ask:

   1. _____

   _____

   2. _____

   _____

   3. _____

   _____

   4. _____

   _____

   5. _____

   _____

GLOSSARY OF TERMS

1. **Balance sheet:** A statement listing the assets, liabilities, and capital structure of a company on a specific date. (See Jamie's Organic Juice Stand Balance Sheet for the format.)

2. **Current assets:** Cash and other assets you can quickly turn into cash, such as accounts receivable and inventory.

3. **Current liabilities:** The debts of a company that are due and payable within the next twelve months.

4. **Deficit:** The money you lost. Time to regroup.

5. **Direct costs:** Costs that can be traced and allocated directly to a specific product, such as the cost of flour in a loaf of bread.

6. **Equity:** The net value of a business, i.e., assets minus liabilities.

7. **Fixed assets:** Assets of a lasting nature such as land, buildings, or equipment.

8. **Fixed costs:** Costs such as rent that don't change in proportion to the level of your sales or production.

9. **Income statement:** A detailed statement showing revenue less all expenses resulting in a net profit or loss for a specific period.

10. **Liquidity:** The degree to which you can produce cash in a short time frame.

11. **Net profit or loss:** Revenue minus all expenses.

Last Words

So there you have it: basic tools for building a business soaked with integrity—one that should complement and strengthen your spiritual progress if I have done my job well. You'll discover that the most efficient way to work through all the guidebook's tasks the first time around is linearly. In other words, you'll need to determine your values and vision for your own life before you sit down to officially work through a business plan. And it really helps to put together the business plan *before* you expend the significant amount of energy that market research will demand. I wouldn't even think about working through a financial budget until I was pretty comfortable with the plan and my market...there are better things you can do with your time. Like meditate or pray. Or play with your kids or clean out your refrigerator.

Once you've worked through the whole workbook, however, you'll discover that, like Indra's net, everything will be interconnected and when one aspect of your business or your life changes, so will everything else. For example, if the market you've identified shifts, you'll want to rethink your business plan. As you rethink your business plan, the financials will be impacted and you may well discover yourself rethinking your vision. Or, your vision for how you want to live your life may change, influencing the size and style of your business, which in turn will have implications for your plan, your market, and your numbers.

The main thing is this: just start. And when things get scary, which they will, have some stories ready that you can tell yourself to remind you that this is all really just a terrific and wildly entertaining three-dimensional game we are playing together. If you need time to collect some stories, here's the one I use when I start to feel unsettled or unsure:

There once was a young monk who went to his teacher in tears. He blurted out that he was having a terrible time with his meditation practice. Every time he settled down, took a deep breath, and closed his eyes, all he could see were two dragons fighting each other. One dragon was a deep blue and it was filled with anger and greed and fear. The other dragon was just as ferocious, only this dragon, a pale luminescent gold, was filled with a fearless wisdom and a deep compassion for all things. Its fire was a deep, deep yellow.

The young man was terrified of what would happen. Which dragon would win? He couldn't tell, and watching them fight terrified him. Could the teacher please give him some advice?

The teacher smiled. He looked at his student, his eyes filled with concern. "You want to know which dragon will win?" The young monk nodded. "Why, the one filled with wisdom and compassion, of course." But how did he know, asked the young monk. "Because that's the one you'll feed," the teacher answered.

So feed your vision and your belief that you can build the business you want and that the world will be a slightly better place for your efforts. Because it's true.